SMART RETIREMENT INCOME

CHRISTINE B. PIERCE

PUBLISHER'S NOTE

This publication is designed to provide information and educational services to the average reader. The author made efforts to ensure that the provided information is accurate, efficient, and reliable. Nevertheless, the author is NOT responsible for omission or errors in the information provided here. The author is also NOT liable for results from the use or misuse of the information provided therein.

INTRODUCTION

"Excuse me! Which of you does not want to grow old?"

I raised my voice all of a sudden as I looked across the room. I have posed this question while I babysat 9-year-olds. I have fired it at a group of teenagers. I have asked adolescents, youths, young adults, and even those already getting into their 40's. I have equally raised it in business dinners, corporate roundtables, and a host of other occasions.

Almost all the times I have raised that question, I got similar answers. Curious eyes peered at me, wondering if I was going nuts. "Is there someone on earth who does not wish to grow old?" they some-times spit. Of course, there are. Several people still commit suicide daily. It may appear absurd to my respondents because they know that life is tough, yet they enjoy every bit of it. They are optimistic and do not even think suicide is an option. So, most of my respondents definitely think it is wonderful to grow old. I bet you are also wondering if there is a real reason you would not want to grow old.

I cannot help my curiosity, however, since you genuinely look forward to growing old, why do you not prepare for old age?

At this point, the message begins to sink in. They exchange glances and begin to realize what I am talking about. A lot of people save a whopping lot of their income for marriage. They save for college, and they save to purchase a home. They keep a big part of their income for vacations. They also prepare for the baby when one is coming. They get a bigger space, work double shifts, and do all sorts to ensure they can provide for the impending situation. Why then do they not adopt the best possible methods to prepare for their retirement?

"I have a social security!" James Baldwin, a smart man once shot back during one of my seminars in the Netherlands. Another person once asked me whether her savings do not qualify as her retirement gratuity. I have met a few others who used the employee 401k or some other archaic method believing that they were saving for retirement. They were indeed saving, however, what they save may just not last beyond their first five years after retirement. I was engaged with a client when it suddenly struck me that many people do not understand the gravity of retirement. It is not just about the money. It is about your health, your comfort, and your fulfillment in the final lapse of your life.

Retirement is not a vacation. It is another life span. It is a time of your life that begins from the 60s' or 70s' (depending on your country's national retirement age) and can span into decades. People still live up to the 90s and 120s. Retirement is a time of your life when you have more time and less energy. You cannot do most of the things you used to, and you cannot compete with 20-year-olds in the workplace. You will only continue to incur basic bills, which will continue for another 30 to 40 years that you have to enjoy before your final lapse. Your actions and inactions at present will determine a lot of what happens at that time. You cannot afford to trifle with that phase of your life.

Just as the anonymous saying goes," the best time to start thinking of your retirement is before your boss does." As early as you can, you must begin to plan for your retirement. You must build your retirement income. It would be best if you built something so comfortable that you can afford to fly your grandchildren down to Tasmania in Australia and stuff them with cookies all at your expense.

You have worked for about 30-40 years of your life, if not more. You should be able to afford what you want when you finally retire. You should never become a liability to your children or the government. You should not find it hard to involve in social activities because you are out looking for what to eat despite working for over 40 years. Social Security will only help you get around the poverty line. It cannot do much if you are looking for a fulfilling retirement where you can travel anywhere or help other people struggling through circumstances. This can only mean one thing - you must prepare for your retirement aggressively.

"How do I do it?" you wonder. "I have an employee 401k; am I on the right track? Do I need to switch my job or save over 60% of my income for retirement?"

Snatch a ballpoint pen and keep the questions flowing. Forget about your age and open your heart. Pen everything you ever want to know about retirement as a successful person. The most exciting news you can have right now is that every imaginable question you may have is already answered in this book. As you go on, you will find practical information on building your retirement wealth. Here and there, you will find answers to every question you may have on generating retirement income. You will also find astute ways of building huge retirement earnings in the age of surging inflation and fast-growing technology.

It does not matter whether you are in your 17's or your 35's. I have documented the steps such that you know how to hop on based on your age, and you will have no trouble building something commendable at the end of your workdays. There is no questioning that the retirement income you can build in your 40s may differ significantly from what you will build in your 20s. Nevertheless, I have structured this book in such a way as to provide you with the information needed to make the best retirement decisions at whatever age this catches you. I met with investment analysts and retirement advisors to ensure I did not miss any critical points. I also met with members at credit bureaus, real estate investment trusts, and several comfortable retirees like Anthony McGill. He led me through the practical ways people can build steady and sufficient retirement incomes.

I only ask that you open your heart and, for a fleeting moment, cast aside everything you thought you knew about retirement planning. You cannot be 100% wrong, but you risk mixing facts with fallacies which can ruin the value of the information you are about to uncover. You also need to get off the Wi-Fi and avoid distractions so you do not miss any critical points. Hop on. Let's ride into the future!

1

WHAT RETIREMENT REALLY MEANS

Congrats on being so tired that you had to retire.

– Anonymous

Before you start reading this book, pull out your phone and dial any contact that comes to mind. The assignment is to ask the receiver, "What do you think retirement means?"

You know what to expect. An average Jack and Joe on the street have an idea of what retirement means. Even if you have just called up a high school student, the chances are that they have a general overview of retirement. So, I cannot present retirement to you as a spanking new initiative that no one has ever heard of.

However, you must understand that complex

circumstances revolve around retirement that most people don't think about. Retirement is not just getting out of work after 40 years. It happens in stages and comes with heavy consequences that you must recognize right from the moment you turn 18. It is okay if you are beyond that and just getting to know. This chapter will expose you to all the stages and implications of retirement.

Just as the quote above suggests, retirement is that time of your life when you are so tired that you have to call it quits. Maybe you are not so tired, but the government and the corporate world believe that you are not the same person who started 40 years ago. You now have weaker bones and a body that can barely do half of what you need. You have become a bank of experience that cannot run a mile a minute in times of emergency. So, you have to ease out of the system and pave the way for the coming generation. As a humanitarian, I see retirement as the most euphemistic way to tell you that you are now an old fellow and you really should take the back seat.

Going by the Merriam-Webster Dictionary definition, "retirement implies withdrawal from one's position or occupation or active working life." In other words, it means to stay away from an active role you have played for the past three to four decades of your life. You switch from skipping breakfast in the morning and joining the early traffic to waking up whenever you like, as though you are on vacation.

The average worker understands that retirement means getting out of work. Moreover, the retiree is considered old, less vibrant, and too fragile to be taken seriously in the workplace anymore. This does not imply that retirement is a terrible condemnation of people who spent their lives working hard, though.

On the flip side, the famous author Bruce Linton believes that "we work all our lives so we can retire – so we can do what we want with our time – and the way we define or spend our time defines who we are and what we value." In essence, retirement should be the plan. It should allow us to go where we want, do what we like, and be ourselves without worrying about work.

The world will have little significance if people never retire. People will keep working when they are no longer agile. Despite having enough to feed their families, they will continue to work and will get no opportunity to actualize their bucket list. Whether you work in a corporate or civil system, retirement is the perfect opportunity to take a step away and see things you would never see if you had to work every day.

Retirement is also the perfect opportunity to take care of your health and be there for your family. By the time an average person is eligible for retirement, they likely experience one or two health conditions. If it is not Type-2 diabetes, it is an ulcer or something else. This may mean they have to slow down and rest more, take more pills, or appear for checkups frequently. Retirement creates time to do just that.

If you are in your 20s or mid-30s, the idea of retirement may not hold water to you because you cannot even imagine how it would happen. But, you should know that it will happen. It will strip you of many resources at your current disposal and offer you a brand new one with a few privileges. Retirement can take another 30 to 60 years of your life. Since you prepare for a new role in a workplace by getting a degree or learning new skills, you prepare for a baby by getting a new home, a bigger space, or even a car for transportation, you cannot afford to face it headlong. You must prepare for it.

According to Wildpine, a Canada-based real estate agency, there are at least 5 phases of retirement. Each one of these phases is crucial to retirement, and we will explore them in the next few paragraphs.

a. The first stage of retirement: The Pre-retirement

The pre-retirement phase is considered the acknowledgment phase. It is that time of your life when you begin to realize that you are not getting any younger. You begin to realize that you are nearing retirement, and you must start to make concrete plans for what is coming.

The pre-retirement is that moment when you realize that building your career further should no longer be your priority. Instead, you must begin to plan for the coming years when you will no longer be at work. You are anxious and excited. You start to look forward to retirement and shift your focus from career growth to financial stability after retirement.

In essence, this is the awareness phase when you start to think your retirement is coming, and you should make plans for it. People make a common mistake: they wait until 5 to 15 years towards retirement before making plans. You may not agree yet, but retiring should be taken into consideration from the day you take up your first job. Your actions and inactions during this phase can shape how the rest of the retirement phases would appear.

b. The second stage of retirement: Full retirement

This phase is also called the honeymoon stage for obvious reasons. It is the moment you have so much anticipated, and you are now officially free. You are free from work, pressure, 9 to 5 routines, and backbreaking deadlines. You don't need long hours and short nights anymore. You need not leave home when you don't want to.

It is also the time when your company makes you feel special with a retirement party, abundance of gifts, retirement cards, compliments, et cetera. You feel more valued and appreciated than you have felt in the past ten years.

It feels so much like a honeymoon, and you enjoy every bit of it. You reconnect with old friends, family, and associates you rarely had time to visit. Some staff members even call occasionally to check up on you. You have enough time to catch up on the TV shows you have missed, the medical checkup you rarely did, and so forth. You may even travel to several places you have always wanted to but could not because you had to be at work. You miss working a bit. But it genuinely feels good to be at home, relaxed, and be recognized as a living legend with a wealth of experience. This is all between 1 and 2 years. After two years, you must proceed to the next stage of your retirement.

I must tell you that some people do not spend their retirement like a honeymoon. After a month or about, they settle into a new routine, business, et cetera. This does not make either right or wrong. It is all about your needs and priorities. We will discuss the smartest way to spend each of your retirement phases in the coming chapters.

c. The third stage of retirement: Disenchantment

This is the phase when the thrill of retiring begins to wear off. You had fantasized about what your retirement would look like from when you were 21. You had more concrete thoughts when you were 45. You even had a closer picture when you were 58. You have anticipated your retirement a whopping lot.

Yet, here you are. You begin to realize at this point that retirement is not much of a deal. Maybe you had too high hopes, or you just didn't feel fulfilled. You begin to feel dissatisfied and uncomfortable. Many a time, you start to feel useless, lonely, and broke.

In this phase, you begin to wonder if you are going to spend the rest of your life doing absolutely nothing. Of course, you have lost some energy before you retire, and you cannot work the way you used to. But you still have some energy, and you have gathered so much experience that it feels wrong to watch them go to waste.

In essence, retirement becomes distressful for most retirees at this phase. There are exceptional situations as always. Some people do not even seem to retire since their life just rolled on even after retirement. But the majority experience this third phase of retirement called disenchantment.

d. The fourth stage of retirement: Reorientation

Reorientation is the rehabilitation phase. It is the point where you realize that things are not working the way they should. You check your bucket list, and you find yourself lagging in all ramifications. You begin to think of how to remain relevant, useful, and fulfilled. You are no longer after tremendous wealth. But you still feel very bored, and you need something to keep you relevant. This is usually the time when people make decisions. They get back to another job. Some choose a local joint to read newspapers every day, others volunteer, et cetera. You can skip the third phase, but unless this fourth phase happens, you will find no meaning in your retirement.

e. The fifth stage of retirement: Reconciliation and Stability

Reconciliation and stability are the best titles for the final stage. At this point, a retiree fully recognizes himself as a retiree. He has experienced the ups and downs of retirement, and he has built some stability. He has already established something that he will likely continue until death. Many retirees even have a routine at this point. They have specific things they eat and places they go to. They sometimes have specific places to socialize or hang out with friends. This explains a lot of patterns observed among older people.

These phases are not easy to scale. You require a lot of money to transition from one to the other. You will navigate between medical bills, boredom, and a struggle to find significance for yourself. On the other hand, you may not even go through some of these phases if you have found enough passion, purpose, and retirement wealth early on. This is why you must extend your pre-retirement planning. In other words, it is best if you begin as soon as possible. To adopt a more practical analysis, here are the key features of retirement.

Key features of Retirement.

a. Retirement means no active work.

By default, retiring implies that you are no longer active at work. You have spent your Monday to Friday at work for decades. You have equally spent a significant part of your weekends preparing for the next week. All of that must stop, and you must find a new purpose for your life. You may also choose to sleep and wake at any time for the rest of your life. Nobody requires you to stay up all night working, and neither do you need to fly from San Francisco to New Orleans.

Officially, you are now as free as a bird. No law explicitly stops you from working in a new environment after retirement. You only retire at a particular place because you have met their retirement specifications. If you look to work in another setting, the chances of getting the same role are slim because every company needs agile and experienced people. And that does not sound like you.

As you would expect, one or two organizations can still use your experience. You may also start a business. So, you are not restrained by law. You are just considered too tired that you need to retire.

b. Retirement also means no pay.

This is one thing everyone sets their hearts upon when they think of retirement. It means you are out of active work, and your salary has stopped for good. While there are pension plans, social security, insurance, and health plans, among other facilities you may be provided, the basic thing is that you will no longer have the big pay you used to have.

On average, salaries range between $55,000-$140,000 per annum in the United States as reported by Ziprecruiter. This puts you between $4,500 and $11,500 each month. When you finally retire, your average social security will range from $1,300-$3,500 if you are in the US (some European countries offer high Social Security). This automatically puts you behind your monthly income.

Transportation and a few expenses may be reduced as you do not have to head to work every day. But you may still have your mortgage (or rent), utilities, club memberships, health subscriptions, and several other bills to pay.

It is disheartening if you have a lot of plans on your bucket list, but you can barely survive, not to mention footing your retirement plans. You may also be ineligible for social security for one or more reasons. So, it is best to think of retirement as a time when you ease out of work with absolutely no pay.

c. Retirement implies that you go back home.

This is obvious, but you must know that retirement is that time you finally go home. To adopt an anonymous tone, "it is that time when your wife thinks she is about to relax because the kids all moved out of the house. But then, you showed up at the door."

In essence, retiring implies that you have plenty of time to spend at home with your family. If the kids haven't moved out, now is the time you argue about football games, the remote control, their education, where they hang out, et cetera. You also have a lot of time with your partner, so there is bound to be plenty of love, bickering, rifts, and communication. If running off to work was your best way to avoid issues in time past, you will need a new strategy when you retire.

Worst, it could result in social exclusion and isolation. You may no longer feel like anyone valued you like they used to. You may feel old, alone, and practically irrelevant. The sequel is a hoard of mental health troubles that can further deplete your health. It does not always happen. But you are at risk as an aged person.

d. Retirement means no traveling allowance or company driver.

It is not just that work is over and the inflow of money has stopped, retirement also strips you of the personal and communal significance you used to have.

You probably had an official driver while you

were at work. You were superior, and you gave directives to people under you. You worked in a nice office, and everyone was always impressed when you told them where you worked and the position you occupied.

Besides your basic salary, you perhaps had bonuses for travel, health, and other situations. You set company goals, handled problems, and collaborated with others. You worked your life out to accomplish a mission that others could not. You pulled deals off with other great guys. You possibly trained mentees who adored your policies and actively learned from you. You were always scared of a particular superior, or you were that superior everyone was scared of. At retirement, all these come to a crashing end.

Unknown to most individuals, these privileges and positions affect their self-esteem and worth. So, while retirement affords more time to spend, there may be an unidentified longing to get that significance anywhere else.

It explains why many aged people seem to go on and on talking about their past, how significant they were, the important things they did when they were younger, et cetera.

e. Retirement means no annual leave, no strikes, no conferences

This is one of the most interesting facts about retirement. While some people were at work, they cringed about how long they had to work. There were hardly any vacations. They had to move from one seminar to the next, depending on the nature of their job. Others also participated in games and dinners organized by their company; they joined staff strikes and explored life in their young years. If you are in your 20s or 30s, you should participate in all of these things because they form the wonderful memories you look back upon when you finally retire. This is to summarize the words of the American entrepreneur, lecturer, and writer, Mark Twain, who warned, "Twenty years from now you will be more disappointed by the things you didn't do than by the ones that you did do."

As a retiree, you will no longer have to attend conferences. There are no protests where you can raise your voice and let adrenaline shoot through you. There are usually few occasions to clap hard and scream, "Yeah!" anymore. You have to understand that retirement promises to be a bore.

f. Retirement means a change of routine.

Retirement means a sudden switch from the lifestyle that has become second nature to you. In the past 30 to 40 years, you have lived in a certain manner and adopted a particular lifestyle. You have woken, slept, drank, eaten, and generally modeled your life after what would suit your occupation. Maybe you even relocated to another city to work in a place with plenty of prospects, and you have been at this for a lengthy period.

You cannot expect yourself to blend so easily into this sudden change. You need time. You are even at an age when adapting to changes does not come easily to you. So, brace up for a whole different life at retirement.

g. Retirement means you have something in your health to think about

According to the World Health Organization, "as people age, they become more susceptible to diseases and disability." The immune system weakens, and the body cannot fight back diseases and infections as it used to. Now is the time you begin to experience the effects of the pills you took, the longer-than-necessary hours you worked, and the excess sugar you consumed, amongst others. If it is not diabetes, it is joint and bone pains, stroke, or a hearing disorder. There are exceptional situations where these things scarcely happen. But they come with the regular old-age package, so you must prepare for one or two of these as you retire.

Additionally, aged people suffer a worse impact than younger ones when abused. It is difficult to stomach financial, verbal, sexual, physical, or psychological abuse from anyone. And all of these are more likely at an older age when one cannot fight back. To speak frankly, someone will assume you are not tech-savvy and may attempt to steal your money digitally. Research even shows that more than half-million elderly individuals aged 65 years and above will experience some form of abuse.

On top of this, the switch from your workplace to a more leisurely role may magnify health problems that have always been there.

h. Poverty

To briefly adopt the words of my favorite author and a former director of Financial Education, Jonathan Clements, "retirement is like a long vacation in Las Vegas. The goal is to enjoy it to the fullest, but not so fully that you run out of money."

Retirement is a part of life that you should look forward to. It is a time when you have a long vacation, and you just sit, watch TV, laugh, and have fun every day like you would during your vacation in Las Vegas. You want to enjoy every bit of it. But the disturbing fact is that your income does not correlate with your expenditure.

As of the end of 2021, Jessica Dickler, a CNBC reporter, noted that "up to 61%" of American adults still live from paycheck to paycheck." Now, take a second and think about that. What happens when the paycheck finally ends? That is the full implication of retirement. You now have the time for your bucket list. The question is how you will have the money. I want you to have both time and money. You should have health alongside. Planning for retirement without thinking of these three is where people get it all wrong. Before discussing the best ways to plan, we will evaluate the things people do wrong in the next chapter.

2

THE UNSPOKEN FACT ABOUT
PLANNING FOR RETIREMENT

To know that you do not know is the best. To think you know
when you do not know is a disease. Recognizing this disease
as a disease is to be free of it. – Lao Tzu

I t was 2010. I had just delivered a speech on
smart money management to a group of Cali-
fornian retirees in the Iconic North Beach Gath-
ering Space. The event was organized by John
Waltz, a nice bloke who led their insurance firm at
that time. After speaking for two hours on the things
you may have done wrong while preparing for
retirement, it occurred to me that everyone looked
sullen.

That realization unsettled me. I had about 24
retirees before me, and I could not understand why

they had seemed excited before I started but now looked at me like I was a ghost. I began to wonder whether I was striking the wrong chord or simply making them uncomfortable. My experience as a financial coach and speaker also reminded me that when people are very impressed, they nod their heads and involuntarily clap.

On this occasion, my group of listeners just looked pale and alarmingly dull. They didn't nod heads or give any outright sign that I was spewing thrash. So, I decided to inquire. I began to move around and ask my audience whether they had made any of the mentioned mistakes. It was at this moment that I realized that everyone in the room had made one mistake or another, and they were gloomy because they realized it could cost them in the coming years. I was surprised, and I made a mental note never to talk about retirement without including the mistakes people make. You must forever avoid these mistakes to have a fulfilling retirement.

This explains the basic reason you are reading this chapter. I have modified these mistakes as the years go by, and the chances are that you will stumble upon one or a few mistakes that never really occurred to you as such. Realizing them can help you identify the things you should never do and things you may have to stop doing when you begin to plan for your retirement. So, off we go in chronological order.

a. Creating no plan at all

Having no plan is the first mistake many people make, which you should not. You only need to look back at your parents and grandparents to realize that you cannot be energetic forever. That time is coming when you just won't have any strength to muster. You cannot work, eat, or do things as you used to. Instead, you have to take a lot of medications, meditate on life, and counsel people if they care.

You might think planning for retirement is so logical that nobody needs to tell anyone. But a study by the U.S. Census Bureau's Survey of Income and Program Participation showed that as of 2017, up to 49% of adults between 55 and 66 are not financially prepared to retire. Check the statistics again and think it over. 49% is about half of people between 55 and 66 years. These people were once energetic youths who didn't need to be reminded to prepare for retirement. Yet, they somehow ended up not financially prepared to retire by 66.

A 2021 study by PwC Retirement also bared that at least 1 in 4 Americans have no retirement savings. Like you, these people all had their 20s, 30s, and 40s, but still ended up with no retirement savings.

b. Not following up on your plans.

It is one thing to map out plans; it is a whole different ball game to back your plans diligently. Of the 49% discussed earlier, at least half of them must have started their lives out with concrete plans. They had ideas of what they wanted to do with their lives. They were confident that they would build an empire and live large by retirement. Some of them even made efforts. But for some obscure reasons, their plans must have fallen through.

This is a key reason you must begin early. If your plans fail, it will happen early, and you can pick your broken pieces up to start all over.

Conversely, if you do not fail, you can begin to reap the benefits right from the moment you are sure you now have enough filed away for retirement. Besides, retirement is not business expansion.

It is neither career development. You must take risks but not to the point where your retirement wealth is jeopardized.

In essence, you must be able to create a concrete retirement framework that can be banked on. And you must be able to manifest the paperwork. You should not just make plans. You should put them on paper and break them into realistic, achievable milestones that begin right from your current age. Your retirement years could extend as long as 30 years. Planning for that moment should begin now.

c. Thinking it is too early.

If you think it is too early to start your retirement plans, you are lying to yourself. You do not just lie to yourself; you also underrate the value and importance of retiring right. Many people leave huge sums for their children even before they grow into adulthood. They create college savings accounts and plan large estates for children under 2. If people can go that far to prepare for kids who still have many years ahead of them, you cannot start your retirement plans too early.

With close to no disadvantages, starting your retirement plans early gives you the leverage to amass a lot in your later years. It allows you to try several things and bounce back if you ever lose. It does not matter whether you earn a little. You will find it easy to continue when you start early. Should you run into a situation that makes it difficult to continue at some point, you will not be badly affected too. For instance, you could develop serious health troubles that put everything on hold. You may also go to jail. Nobody likes these circumstances, but the future is so far off that there is plenty of time for many unexpected things to happen.

When you start early, you will still have something to fall back on if you bounce out of that disruptive circumstance after some years rolled by. Your best insurance is getting started early.

Some people say that quitting your job can disrupt your retirement plans. But this is not necessarily true, especially if you are young. You can seamlessly move on to bigger prospects or start something else that affords you enough to increase your retirement income at the end of the day. Building a retirement plan should not hold your world to a standstill. The important thing is kicking off on the right foot and doing it early.

d. Using a savings account

Using a savings account is one of the average people's biggest mistakes when planning for retirement. Nobody may have told you this, but using the traditional savings account to prepare for retirement is the most impracticable retirement plan anyone could have. It suggests that you are saving for three to five years after retirement. You are not saving so that you will never have to work for the next thirty years after retirement.

It isn't smart enough. And you must thrash that idea if that was your initial retirement plan. Chapter six will discuss everything that is not right about using the traditional savings account to prepare for retirement.

We will also head on to more practical ways to save such that the value of your savings will be preserved, and you will get more substantial compound interests.

e. Treading the wrong path of risk

Risk is the most sensational aspect of your retirement finances. It is directly proportional to wealth. The higher your risks, the higher the tendency to make or break you. If you take extremely high risks, you increase your chances of winning more. You also stretch your safety and expand your chances of poverty. If you take too few risks, you limit the chances of growing sufficient wealth and reduce the possible loss rate.

You cannot take the same level of risk on your retirement savings as you would on wealth-building initiatives. During your younger years, you can choose to mortgage your home to get money to expand your business. You can quit your job to get a better one or choose to start a business. But on no account should you mistakenly take such a level of risk on your retirement investment.

You need steady, progressive, and assuring retirement plans. That is the smart investment key that most people do not realize.

f. Delaying Debt

Debt generally refers to every amount of money you draw on other companies or organizations with the belief that you would refund it over time. It could be a token amount you got from a friend. It could also be substantial, like your credit card loans, mortgage, or education loans.

Whatever it is, delaying debt is one of the common complications that result in heavy consequences. In typical situations, a loan comes with the agreed interest. This interest is bound to increase Year on Year. Loans like mortgages and student education loans are a lot, and they can heavily eat at your retirement investment if you do not clear them till retirement.

Becoming a senior does not also wipe off your credit records. The credit card companies require funds to continue operations, and your debt increases as you delay it. These situations can heavily affect how much you eventually have as your retirement funds.

g. Not taking advantage of work policies.

One of the most exciting features of the 21st-century workplace is that companies make various provisions for their staff. The bigger your company gets, the more provisions are available for employees.

Companies like Google do not just stop at benefits. If an employee dies while at work, the surviving spouse or partner will acquire vested stock benefits, and their children will receive $1,000 a month until the age of 19.

Many companies partner with utility providers, health organizations, auto dealerships, and so on to enable their staff members to access the products and services at subsidized rates. While you may have enough to purchase at the standard rate, it is economical to use these packages provided at subsidized rates. Aside from the fact that it reduces your overall cost, it also affords you more money to reserve in your retirement account.

Many employees cut themselves short by not taking advantage of their company's retirement provisions. They neglect the pension funds, insurance agencies, cashback policies, free medical checkups, and other long-term benefits. They believe they have enough money to create a package for themselves. So, they care little about the health and retirement offers their company may set up.

This may include the popular 401k and other pension options you may have in your community. If you are one of those who assume these health insurance packages are for low-level staff and you have enough to take care of yourself, you may be barking on the wrong horse.

h. Taxes

Assuming that you are smarter than taxes is another foolish mistake you must never make. Many people commit this blunder, and they pay heavily at a time when it is too late to make amends. This is why it is sometimes ideal to stick to post-tax savings than pre-tax.

Assuming you do not get the hang of what I am pointing out, here is a simple way to look at it. Across the United States and Europe, the government recognizes people's desire to save for retirement. So, they often initiate several retirement plans and packages for the employees.

Some of these retirement plans are tax-deferred, meaning that you are charged nothing in tax all through the period you save. Your money continues to grow until you finally decide to pull it out at retirement. This is when you will be required to pay the applicable tax. An example of such retirement packages is the 457(b) plan in the United States and Ireland. The basic problem is that you might lose sight of the fact that you are yet to pay tax or underestimate how significantly your tax might eat out of your savings. So, you just assume your saving is "$150,000," and you feel confident that you have something you can look forward to.

i. Not investing enough in the future.

As seen in the statistics provided by the US Census Bureau at the start of this chapter, too many people do not invest enough in the future. If you pick a group of people in their 20s in a random study, it is rare to find anyone who doesn't understand that they will grow old and unenergetic at some time in their lives. The same is true of those in their 30s and 40s. It then makes it quite disturbing that despite this level of awareness, about one of every 2 seniors is not prepared to retire.

Some even retire too early because they are tired of working, and some pull out of their retirement funds. After all, they are confident that they will work hard, earn enough and never have to worry about their old age because they would reel in millions.

It is lovely to have dreams, but you must understand that every dream requires some level of realistic sacrifice. You should have something in the coffers that neither hunger nor your risk appetite should prompt you to withdraw. It is one thing to put something in the coffers; it is a whole different ball game to understand that this is not a reserve account for emergencies. It is a reserve for another phase of your life.

j. Planning to retire late

Planning to retire late is the reason many people do not save enough in the early years. They hope they'd go on into their 70s and more. They believe they could keep grinding till they suffer a stroke or a terminal condition. They detest the idea of going home to do nothing when there is something they have been passionate about for the past few decades.

So, first off, they believe they will continue to make money. They also assume it might take some time before they resort to the retirement reserves, so they only contribute tidbits to the retirement stockpile. Moreover, people like these do not quickly shift focus from career development to retirement development.

The full implication is that they are knocked off balance when their company turns them home or a government policy mandates that they retire before their intended age. It is worst when they have to return due to a health condition of some sort. Not only would they have to stop earning money, they will be forced to spend the insufficient amount of money that may have been set aside for retirement on salvaging their health.

You can plan to retire late. But that should not slow down your retirement savings. That simple principle can set you off to a fulfilling retirement. On the flip side of the coin, some people retire too early, and it bounces on their retirement gratuity.

If your total retirement package was $100,000 when you retired in your 50s, it could have gone up to $120,000 if you had waited till your 60s, and your total expenses for about ten years would be out of your retirement needs. This is the most practical way to let you know that planning to retire too early or too late can upset your retirement balance.

k. Paying incessantly high bills

The sensational coach and author, Robert Kiyosaki once warned, "It is not about how much money you make. It is about how much money you keep." In other words, it is not about sitting at the oval office of your company and getting the fattest chunk of the check. It is about how much of it you are about to reserve at the end of the day.

This simple principle comes into play when you examine your finances. While tipping off the waiter, taxi driver, and so forth is a sign of generosity, you increase your expenses with every tip-off. You shoot your bills higher, and you slash your total net worth. Many things should not incur the high bills you pay for them and you know it. You may not realize how much they affect your finances at an instant. But you should know that you can put your financial balance in better shape if you do not spend on incessant things because they appear attractive.

Much importantly, you must avoid incurring high bills on your retirement operations. This means that your retirement investment portfolio should be managed by a professional whose charge is decent. That way, your management fee is subsidized and you will not pay an outrageous percentage when the management charge is deducted.

1. Divorce

In a 2020 Journal of Marriage and Family, Nicole Kapel and Janeen Baxter found that "personal wealth tends to decline substantially following separation, and rarely recovers after divorce." Much more than both parties expected, couples often lose a chunk of their wealth during a divorce. One party is bound to forfeit the home, car, truck, or other joint assets. They will both lose money on the legal processes. One party will also have to spend much more than their usual expenses on child support.

On top of that, they are emotionally damaged and unmotivated to go further and amass their wealth. This is by no means a recommendation that you sit back and fold your arms in an unhappy marriage. But you should try to fix it if you can, rather than hurriedly scramble for a way out.

Find a place in your memory to preserve the words of the famous journalist and author, Mitch Albom who said that "In college, I took a Latin course, and one day the word divorce came up. I always figured it came from some root that meant divide. In truth, it comes from the Latin word, *divertere*, which means to divert. I believe that. All that divorce does is divert you."

m. Skipping paperwork

Skipping paperwork is a simple yet significant

behavior that can cost you heavily in the future. To a layman, paperwork refers to documentation, signature, and other processes that show that something is legal and binding. This could be an agreement, a loan deal, car dealership, mortgage, emergency fund management, next of kin dealings, and so many others.

Skipping any of the aforementioned paperwork may not seem important to you at the instance. But any of them could easily lead to problems that jeopardize your retirement in the coming years. By way of illustration, assume that you failed to properly document a loan you gave to an individual, if he refuses to pay, or he dies, you will be forced to pay for it as you will have no way to prove to his family that he owed you a penny.

This illustration may seem mild and non-consequential. But several things may punch holes in your retirement plans because they were not properly documented. Your car dealership might be trying to pull a fast one on you so you pay again. Incurring losses from such deals reduce the amount you can save for your retirement. I found that many people often skip one or two of their paperwork and they often get away with it. Nobody promises that you can be that lucky.

n. Gambling

The funniest and most realistic description of gambling was given by the American captain, Jack Yelton. To him, "the easiest way to return from a casino with a small fortune is to go there with a large one." Reflecting on that statement helps you understand that gambling is a palace where fortunes are eaten up. It is a game of luck, meaning that it is extremely risky and you can lose your life-long saving in it. You will lose some and win some and your losses can displace everything you have reserved all your life.

You are even more likely to lose than win, and the addictive tendency of gambling helps nothing. You will continue to go back and again till you have nothing even in reserve. Gambling will reduce the amount you have to spend on yourself and other basic needs. It can plunge you into depression and addiction. It can eliminate your sense of savings and preservation. You cannot think of productive ways to earn money because you are looking for "quick wealth." A perspective like this does not help your retirement investment at all.

Over and above, you must genuinely under-stand that many mistakes can disrupt your retirement plans. It is okay to constantly modify your plans for the better. But no matter how young you are, you must begin to prep for retirement. Getting married, working menial jobs and other similar situations should not be your excuse.

Now that we know precisely what we need to avoid, let's tear apart the most important thing everyone looks forward to when they think of retirement: retirement income.

3
RETIREMENT INCOME: THE NUTS AND BOLTS

I assume I must have a pension, but I don't know for sure. I have heard of ISAs, but I can't tell you if I have any. – Ian Gillan

In its most basic sense, retirement income is an umbrella phrase for every source of income generated upon retirement. In essence, it refers to the ways people generate money when they are no longer in a salaried job. Much before your retirement, your salary was certainly your essential source of income. Whether you worked for the government, a private entity, or yourself, your expenditure was primarily sorted by the direct income you got from your hard work. Now that you are "too tired" to work, your sources of income are all classed as retirement income.

Your sources of income at this point may be something you have started in the past, an investment that begins to yield at this point, or a new venture you are attempting to guarantee stable income all through your retirement. The central idea behind this book is to help you realize the most innovative and most realistic retirement income that can help you adjust to life after retirement. So, you can be sure that we will address this aspect impressively.

Before that, you must understand that there is a common mistake people make, and you need to avoid it. Many investment advisors and retirement managers convince people that they need a specific amount in their retirement purse. They pressure them to save this amount or spend that amount before retirement. They woo them into believing they need $ 1 million or $40 million before retiring. So, people begin to pressure themselves to attain this amount. I am here to tell you that sticking with an available amount is the biggest flop you can ever have in your retirement plan.

It sounds ordinary. But it is largely unwise to

save a general amount. It is never about how much you have been able to save at retirement. It is a question of how much you need at retirement. Some people have cleared their mortgage, and they have no auto debts. They also have no credit card debts, and neither do they have overdrafts from any bank. There is almost nothing unchecked on their bucket list, and they are not interested in flying around in old bones. People in this category will require little to maintain themselves when they finally retire. With their 401(k) and social security, they may be well off than several others who took loans.

On the flip side, life will be significantly different for anyone who belongs to the group of seniors who are not financially ready to adapt. They probably still have a mortgage to clear. They still have a long-standing debt and plenty of unmarked desires on their bucket lists. They clearly need a lot more than the former retiree we pointed out. So, they should not be encouraged to save the same amount.

In essence, your prospective lifestyle will heavily determine how much you should look to reserve for your later years. By saving for retirement, you are trying to generate income that can last you for a significant period long after you are out of work and taxes have been deducted from your retirement income.

Traditionally, these are the most popular ways to generate retirement income. After discussing these basics, I need to show you the major types of retirement income. We will, of course, consider the most innovative retirement income strategies down to the end of this book.

Pension

In the words of the award-winning founder and CEO of Sensible Money, Dana Anspach, "pension is a retirement plan that provides a monthly income. The employer bears all the risk and responsibility for funding the plan." A pension is a retirement plan that guarantees some monthly income for anyone retiring. The astonishing thing about it is that it is managed by the employer, not the actual person in whose name the trust is created.

You can think of a pension as a salary you get after leaving work. It is still paid by your former employer (whether government or private agency), and you get it every month till you pass. The difference from your original salary is that it is significantly smaller, and you are no longer required to be at work. In some cases, your company may decide to offer you this retirement fund as a one-time lump sum.

Ordinarily, most government agencies provide pensions to their workers. You are only required to meet a certain age and service specification before you are eligible. For instance, 35 years in service or 66 years of age is the general condition in the US as of 2022. The age varies in the UK but is usually around 66 years.

You need to verify what the terms are in your country. So, you should consult a local pension office or call your administrative secretariat. Your colleagues in the government agency can also direct you to the appropriate quarters for clarifications.

In private entities, this situation is a little bit tweaked. The United States does not mandate employers to provide retirement plans for employees, while countries like the United Kingdom mandate retirement plans for all employees. This again reminds you that there is no one way to look at this. While the concept is similar, the governing policies may be different.

So, you can work with a private company in the United States and never have a retirement pension set up by your company. If it wasn't mentioned in your employment terms, it is best to ask. This is because your company may have skipped that part since you are a complete newbie, and you need to have met some conditions before you access the package.

Also, they may have jumped it altogether because it does not exist in their plans, and you need to know that early. While a retirement pension may not suffice as enough excuse to quit a workplace, it makes sense to understand what the company has in store for old staff members so you can plan your retirement around it.

Depending on the policies and the situation, some pensions can be transferred to a spouse or next of kin. Some others grow with the inflation rate of the country.

Pension also has a general formula: Years of Service multiplied by the final average salary and multiplied by the multiplier. Your final average salary refers to your average monthly earnings while the 'multiplier' is a value that determines the fraction of your final average salary that will be paid to you as your retirement benefit. For instance, with a multiplier of 2% (0.02), a person who worked for 25 years with a final average salary of $70, 000 would get a pension of 25 x 2% x $70, 000 = $35, 000.

Retirement income in the United States is regulated by the Employee Retirement Income Security Act (ERISA.)

401 (k)

According to Dana Anspach, pension is not the only retirement income a company may create for its staff members. A private company may also consider the much popular 401(k.) If this sounds foreign to you, 401(k) is a retirement plan also sponsored by the employer. The primary difference is that 401(k) is designed such that the employer and the employee contribute to the account. It is not just the employer who contributes a percentage of the employee's salary to the retirement account as in pension.

In other words, pension centers around a defined benefit plan while 401(K) centers around a defined contribution plan. By defined benefit, I imply that the benefit of the package to the employee is immediately apparent. While you cannot access the funds until you have reached an agreed age and specification, you already know how much your company contributes each month. You also know the sum to expect at the end of the day.

On the other hand, a defined contribution plan suggests that your benefit is not fixed at the end of the day. What is fixed is that if you contribute a given percentage to this retirement wallet, your company donates a percentage too. This percentage is usually agreed upon before time.

As illustrated by Margaret James, the CEO of Peggy James, CPA, PLC, your employer may offer a 50% match of your contributions to your 401(k) up to 6% of your salary. This means that if your salary sits around $100,000, and you contribute $6000, which is 6% of your income, to your 401(k), your employer must add 50% of your contribution being $3000. So, you have a defined contribution plan here. Your contribution to the retirement plan determines your eventual benefit; since your company will always add 50% once you save about 6% of your income. In some situations, your employer may add a profit-sharing feature to the deal so they will own a quota of what you make with your investments.

Over and above, everyone finds out that a pension is insufficient for what they wish to achieve at the end of the day. While the average pension sits around $10000 annually, an average household may require up to $5000 or more to keep the family going each month.

The 401(k) was initially set up to support pension so you can have enough money when you finally retire. But slowly, it has replaced pension in private organizations. Over 85% of companies that set up retirement plans for their employees prefer to use the 401(k.) That tells you to expect 401(k) or something close should you switch to a private company.

Besides 401(k) and pension, the two most popular sources of income for retirees are social security and 403(b.)

403 (b)

The 403(b) plan is incredibly close to the 401(k), except that it does not usually comply with a lot of the regulations in the ERISA, while the 401(k) does. To start with, 403(b) is also an employer-sponsored plan. You create a retirement account where the employer automatically pays an amount every month. The caveat is that the money is paid from your primary salary, not your employer's wallet. It is often adopted by tax-exempt organizations like government agencies, publicly owned institutions, and NGOs, not private organizations. Professionals like teachers, doctors, nurses, and civil servants in tax-exempt institutions often use this.

In some cases, your firm may offer to contribute a match as in the 401(k), but they don't in a typical situation. Because it is your money, the ERISA is not very strict on the regulations guarding your use of the capital, except that they have a standard limit you can save annually. Also, there is a limit to the investment options available to you.

With regards to taxes, you can choose the regular option or the ROTH. The standard option allows you to save for retirement before tax. This means taxes are charged when you withdraw at retirement. ROTH, contrastingly, means that you save after-tax. So, whatever you save and the yield is all yours. There is no significant difference except that 401(k) is sponsored from the employer's wallet, and 403(b) is from your savings.

IRA

This is the same system known as ISA in the UK and IRA in Australia. IRA is an acronym for Individual Retirement Account. As the name suggests, it is an individual account you set up yourself, just like a regular checking or savings account. And it is set up in a financial institution like a bank, mutual fund, stock brokerage, or life insurance firm. It can be tax-deferred or ROTH (Tax-free) like the earlier options, and you can roll over your funds from other investment options.

When IRA was started, the idea was to supplement your other retirement savings with something a bit broader. This looks necessary because several experts have observed that retirement plans like 401(k) and social security still do not meet the needs of people upon retirement. People need approximately 85% of their current income to live comfortably during retirement. So, they have to supplement their retirement income with other funds and investments. Unlike the different retirement plans, IRA provides access to broader investment choices and the tax rate is significantly lower when measured with other options.

Social Security

Social security is another way people typically generate retirement income. It is an income system designed by the government to support aged citizens and those who have some natural disabilities.

So, it is for retirement and survivor benefits. If you live in the United Kingdom, you will find a similar system in the National Insurance Scheme.

Usually, the system is so accommodating that your spouse and even ex-spouses can become eligible. It is all based on your earning records while you were actively working. You can set up a social security tax if you are self-employed when you file your federal tax returns. Employees pay through a system known as payroll tax which processes cuts from your income and reserves them for your Medicaid or Social Security. While this income is guaranteed, it is significantly smaller than all others we have earlier identified.

Inheritance

Inheritance is the most convenient means to become wealthy upon retirement. As you probably guessed, it is that accumulation of real estate properties, cars, and financial assets passed on to you by someone who shares your genetic information. That could be your parent, uncle, cousin, or grandparents. Today, inheritance is grand to the point where a friend can list you as part of their survivors and beneficiaries should they die.

The government does not usually tax inheritance. They only tax you when you generate profit from it. For instance, no government will charge for the $100,000 passed on to you by your parents. But they will tax you when you pump that into a real estate or investment. You don't need an employer to be eligible for inheritance from all indications. You only need to survive someone who has written you among their survivors and beneficiaries list. In a typical situation, people write how they want their properties shared upon demise. Where this is not applicable because there are crises or the deceased did not prepare a will, governments worldwide have specific measures of determining how the inheritance is shared. If your spouse becomes deceased, they may leave so much property that upon retirement, you have something to live on. Such situations make inheritance a possible source of income.

Home equity

Home equity is the percentage of ownership you have on your house. It is the total percentage you own when your mortgage is dedicated. For instance, you have 100% home equity if you have completely paid off your mortgage, and you have

60% home equity when your home costs $500000, of which you have paid a sum of $300000. With this, you can take a lump sum of $300000 as your home equity, and then refund a fixed amount monthly. This is not a permanent source of income. It is a loan you must repay within a specified period. You can pull for this during retirement, and the fact that it allows you to start a business makes it an intelligent retirement revenue option.

From the start of this chapter, I have exposed you to the process most people go through. The system is concrete, and most people are stuck in the cubicle. We have been conditioned to the things we can and cannot do all our lives. We have been told to get to school and graduate (with or without loans), get a job, apply for a credit card, and go after an auto loan which should then be followed by a mortgage (especially if you are lucky to clear your student debt early).

Sometimes, marriage and children come in, couple that with your rentals, utilities, and groceries, and you will have enough bills to pay for the rest of your life. Your best shot may be to stay stuck in your job, like it or not. Many people are sandwiched between a couple of jobs to ensure they foot their bills and survive. To ensure they end up with something in their grey days, they save into IRA and the other retirement options discussed earlier.

At the end of the day, it is disturbing to hear the National Institute of Retirement Security report that as of 2020, up to 40% of seniors rely on Social Security for survival. This is about $1558.54 each month. It sounds like a lot until you remember the Bureau of Statistics states that an average senior household requires $3800 to pull through each month. The average pension is around $2250 per month, and there are still chances of rising inflation. Piece it all together, and you can then decipher why many still cannot afford to tick off their bucket list at retirement despite working so hard in their youth. They struggle to survive, and some still take on odd jobs. What about those that are not qualified for social security? What about those who have no pension?

The implication is glaring.

You need a standard income if you plan to be comfortable in retirement. You need something that allows you to sleep, go on trips, and never worry about debts and financial troubles. These traditional retirement options even have saving limits, so there is a limit to how comfortable you can get at retirement through them.

This means what?

You need something out of the box. You need a legitimate and exceptional strategy to beat the old-age poverty game. That strategy should either auto-generate income or require close to no effort to do it. And it should be very reliable when your bones become so old that you have to clear out your office desk. When you finally strike that thing, you need to start working on it.

Many people think the entire idea may sound like a wild goose chase because they are subconsciously held back in the cubicle. They believe ventures beyond the typical saving and retirement plans are not genuine or might be extremely risky. You must dump such mindsets in the can as you further in the book. The strategies in this book are highly efficient. Also, several personalities that I will randomly mention as I discuss the strategies have tried them and found them reliable. Before we head on to that, let us discuss the debts you may incur at retirement as we have batted around the sources of income for a retiree.

4
DEBT AND RETIREMENT
TAXES WAITING FOR YOU

To look and feel my best, I watch my calories and exercises
-Kim Kardashian.

W ait a minute! We have been talking about retirement income all along. What about liabilities? Have we suddenly forgotten that the entire spectrum revolves around liabilities? Potential debts, retirement taxes, and expenses are vital factors that can make or mar your retirement investments. They can determine how much you save, how much you need, and how much financial trouble you may have when you retire. So, we will extensively explore debts and retirement taxes.

Recently, the Canadian finance agency; Sun Life conducted a survey that found out that up to a quarter of Canadian retirees are in one form of debt. Similarly, the Senior Living Organization believes that of ten older adults in the US, eight are in one form of debt at least. In a recent survey, the personal finance writer Jessica Dickler verified that 46% of American respondents expect to retire with debts. These are glaring pieces of evidence that retirement is from work, not from bills.

Where is the bliss we were all hoping for upon retirement? How can anyone sleep soundly with the realization that debts are hanging over their heads, coupled with the constant reminder that they are now too weak to get a job and their current income is scarcely sufficient to cover monthly expenses? That definitely was not the anticipated retirement anyone dreamed of. To see what you might easily trim off before retirement, we must review these debts.

Common Retirement Debts

Credit Card

While it is incredibly petite than the others, credit card debt is the most frequent debt incurred by seniors across America. It is easy to understand.

A credit card gives you the feeling that you can have what you want right now and pay sometime in the future. "It is just a pair of jeans," "it is just $10," or "I still have my job, and I can foot this later", many people say, motivating themselves to pile up their expenses with a flimsy excuse and a shady conviction.

So, lots of people develop the habit of purchasing things they can't instantly afford. Mismanaged, this debt continues into retirement. Sometimes, it is not just the debt - the practice of buying what you can't afford continues as well. This lack of financial discipline is why several seniors incur debts they cannot pay till their demise. Such obligations are extracted from their properties, making inheritance a not-so-reliable wealth source. In plain English, don't overly count on it if you have a relative who can leave you with surplus wealth upon demise. Of course, unless you are sure of how much debt they have incurred.

In a 2020 study by the Senior Living Organization, up to 52% of seniors who are in debt admit theirs is a credit card debt. Considering the general populace, about 55% of debts in the US are Credit Cards, so the differences are tiny, except that we are comparing people who work with those who may not be able to work, even if they try to.

There is a big clue here for you. If you have credit card debt at present, the statistics show that you are likely to carry that debt into retirement. Now that you see this coming, you can avoid it by changing your approach to spending on credit cards and clearing off the debt you have left. It is not as easy as it sounds, of course. But you should cut any bill you can to guarantee what grants you peace of mind on your last lap. Many adults didn't take that decision when they had a more robust immune system and better ability to withstand adverse conditions. Now, in their fragile days, some are often caught skipping meals and pills just to make sure they foot their bills and don't return to the street to beg.

Mortgage

Currently, the mortgage is the next highest debt that spans into retirement in the United States. Everyone wants a home. The idea of renting despite working for over 30 years is unappealing, and it is also a poor decision financially. People also have personal and professional motivations for signing up for a mortgage. Eventually, they enroll in 10, 15, 20, or even 30-year payment packages.

The standard practice is to consider the number of years you have before retirement, your marital status and current expenses, and other critical factors before signing up for a package. These factors should help you pick a package that offsets your bills by retirement. But for some reason, this is not always the case.

Of all respondents in the Senior Living Organization Survey, 41% admit to having mortgage bills despite retiring. This seems a lot since a mortgage can take anywhere between 10 to 30 years to clear on a monthly payment of over $1400, and you may still have years to go. It gets complex when you remember that up to 92% of seniors develop at least one health condition by retirement. So, they often have to spend on medication, groceries, and pay utilities (though subsidized in some instances). Their financial structure leaves only a tiny room to spend on a mortgage.

41% is a significant figure. It suggests that about one in every two persons is likely to end up in mortgage debt. To ensure you do not fall into such debts, you must have cleared your mortgage before retirement. You should make this a priority if your financial structure allows you to. However, understand that you are not alone if you cannot seamlessly do this because you are underemployed, divorced, or in a serious financial predicament. You may use the reverse mortgage option, which allows you to get equity on your home, spend the money, and remain in the house till you move or become deceased. The house is no longer yours, but you are not shoved out until you move. You can also consider smart consolidation loans. Rather than skip medications or meals at old age, you should seriously consider the retirement investment options discussed in this book.

Liabilities

Liability is a complex term in many disciplines. Here, it refers to every bill you incur due to your association with somebody. In essence, it is a sum-up of bills you incur due to your commitment and responsibility to people around you. This starts from your brother and sisters to your parents, friends, in-laws, spouse, and, more importantly, your children.

You are not liable to anyone by default. But you are sometimes connected such that you may have to lend them some money which might turn into bad debt. You may also give money to people, foot their medical bills, or repair their vehicles because they have no insurance. Liability may also refer to a corporate loan you have drawn in your name and are liable for, whether or not you are at work.

When it is none of this, it might be an organization to which you pledged financial commitment. It goes as far as a gym, an NGO, a Go-Fund-Me, a vegetarian society, a political party, a racial or religious movement, et cetera. They are all liabilities, and you should not expect them to automatically stop because you are now taking a back seat at work.

Presumably, you assume you can quickly call off all submissions upon retirement. You figure you might ring them and tell them you can no longer financially back their movement. Or maybe you think you might just cut down the amount you spend on them each month. It sounds pretty simple in theory but might be difficult to achieve in reality. You have a vested interest in the organization and have backed them for 5, 10, or even 20 years of your life. Now that you have all your time to yourself, you may become melancholic when you realize that retirement has stripped you of the economical relevance you have enjoyed in the organization. It might even be shameful to announce that you can't do so much anymore. What some people do is that they keep going, and their expenses pile up.

Auto loans

Auto loans come as the next most significant loan on the list. Approximately 34% of Senior Living Survey respondents claim that they have an auto loan. This rate is 10% lower than the average in the active age range. It is relatively easier to pay off an auto loan compared to other debts, but it still requires commitment and sacrifice. Sometimes, that could be to your detriment.

Another survey highlights seniors often put on hold basic car repairs due to their financial situation, just like the pills and nutrition they sometimes skip. The implication is that their vehicle can get messy and result in an accident, which is considered one of the leading causes of death among seniors. If you are near retirement and not on an auto loan yet, it is more thoughtful and financially wiser to lease a car than take an auto loan. However, if you are in it, you still need one of the many options we will talk about.

Taxes

Tax is not in the record of most people because they believe retirement income is ultimately theirs. My empirical studies certify that this is far from the truth in most cases. Ultimately, your retirement income is yours only when you save through a ROTH retirement plan or other plans that encourage post-tax saving. Otherwise, you must credit Uncle Sam when you eventually withdraw your retirement income.

There are several tax benefits for seniors in the US, as you probably guessed. But these tax benefits are primarily for people who earned amounts that will likely not suffice for their basic survival needs. Practically, there are specific reasons you may not qualify. If you invest in stocks or start a business upon retirement, you must expect to pay taxes too. So, when you plan your investment payments, you must include tax.

Medical bills

There are bound to be other debts but this is the last that we can easily put the finger on. The national council on aging recently published that about 80% of seniors are battling one or more health complications. Three-quarters even have at least one chronic condition that requires them to live on pills or principles for the rest of their lives. If it is not diabetes, it is stroke, dementia, or a physical injury.

To maintain such conditions, they need to check themselves at the clinic frequently. They have insurance and social security plans, but they soon find out that these plans do not suffice for their medications, so they often have to pull out of their retirement income.

Only 13% claim to have incurred such debts in the Senior Living Organization Survey respondents but the rate is not the point. The point here is that medical debts are one such you can incur in the final chapter of your life. You cannot pay this off before retirement, like an auto loan or mortgage. It is even trickier to fix an amount because you cannot tell how much medication you will require when the time comes. What you can do is have enough to foot your bills, whatever it is.

From all indications, there are hardly any new debts. It is the same old debts you may have incurred because of a lack of financial discipline or underemployment. I must point out that most debts that span into retirement are consumer debts. Consumer debt is an umbrella term for all debts generated on personal maintenance. Credit cards are mainly used to purchase tickets, meals in a restaurant, gas, online items, and other consumer products. It is not education, business, or investment.

The consequence of these debts on your retirement

a. Retiring in peace is a mirage

Retiring is one of the most sensational moments in most people's lives. They keenly look forward to the time they can sit back, compete with their grandkids for the TV remote, and never have to worry about working. Retirement is the opportunity to babysit for your children while they work and tell your grandchildren stories of the world.

Such sceneries cannot manifest if you are anxious, depressed, or overly stressed about money. You cannot make time for anyone; neither will you have the mental and psychological balance a typical retiree should have. You may even put your health and mental wellness on the line, increasing your medical bills and adding to your worries.

b. You may forfeit some properties.

Depending on how much debt you have to serve and your repayment system, you may forfeit some of your legacies. An auto loan dealership may take the car when you cannot pay because your rationed income is spent on medical bills or another imminent financial situation.

In complex cases, you may lose properties you have worked hard to accumulate. This is more likely in cases where you listed such properties as collateral or were dragged to court and filed for insolvency. If you have low equity on your home, you must promptly make your payments or risk losing your home.

c. Retirement may not turn out to be retirement for you.

In the middle of these crises and debts, retirement is a mirage. The circumstances may compel you to pick up a new job, start a go-fund-me, or rely on family and friends. Your vacation is based on how kind your relatives choose to be. And you may struggle to afford medication in the midst of growing medical conditions.

The system deemed you unable to keep going at the rate you used to. That was the real reason you retired. Now that you are growing weaker, inactive, and less productive, taking up a new job is more challenging. First, everyone is looking for young and energetic people who can sit through the hours tirelessly. It is also to your detriment because you may still look and feel agile. Still, there are pieces of scientific evidence that stress will improve your blood pressure and cholesterol level and impair your cognitive performance. You are only putting your health and mental safety on the line.

d. Your bucket list will remain unfulfilled.

It hurts to see that you have worked so long and still reek of liabilities; a situation like that can plunge you into depression. You work hard, yet you are only going about in circles. Beyond depression, anyone can do themselves in because they feel like the world has been unfair to them.

Besides the personal debts we discussed earlier, you may owe a few friends, your spouse, or an uncle in a non-official capacity. It is all debt, and depending on the arrangement, it can span into retirement. A steady pension or social security can help you live by the day, but you will have a hard time if you run into most of these debts. You can easily avoid them, except for the likes of medical expenses, which is highly likely. The harsh reality is that Go-fund-me works better to save children and citizens in warring countries. Your children also have costs to cover. So, the one person who can take you and your bills seriously is you. And you must prepare from now.

5
WHY YOU MUST GET AHEAD WITH RETIREMENT INCOME

Don't dig your grave with your own knife and fork.
—Old English Proverb

I have dropped hints here and there all through the previous chapters. We will extensively discuss the benefits of setting up a substantial retirement income.

a. Income must happen at retirement.

The first reason you need to get a concrete plan for your retirement is that income must happen. You have only been eased out of your job; you still have bills to pay. Several dreams and responsibilities require money to actualize. You may have some pension or 401k, but you probably understand now that such retirement plans cannot foot your bills over a long period. You still need groceries, gas in your car, and repairs on your roof, among other things. It would help if you had something sufficient, steady, and entirely reliable.

b. It allows you to keep funding your liabilities.

As defined by the Oxford dictionary, a liability is something for which you are responsible and is sometimes backed by law. On average, most people are not responsible for their kids by retiring. But they are still responsible for several other things. For instance, you may be responsible for your spouse's welfare. You may also be responsible for an organization, NGO, club, et cetera. Sometimes, you have financial obligations to them. At other times, you have activities you have assured you will carry out. You cannot be available for either of these if you have financial problems to worry about constantly. Sometimes, no law mandates you to do it; it is just personal pride and ethics. Whatsoever it is, you want to be able to foot your liabilities.

c. Less liability to anyone

To adopt the words of the award-winning author Frank Sonnenberg, "dependency purges people of their dreams, makes their spirit atrophy, and enslaves them to a lifetime of mediocrity."

Having spent up to two-quarters of their lives working tirelessly, no senior should be purged of their dreams. You should not end up enslaved to the whims and discretion of people, especially regarding your finances. Whether you are 20 or 40, you must never forget that you command more respect if you are financially well off at retirement.

d. You can retire early.

Most people do not retire until 70 because they need their retirement package to contain a substantial amount. Already, they are burned out and exhausted at work. If you can scale that hurdle by building a reliable, steady, and sufficient income, you can retire early with no regrets.

While everybody, including the social security agencies, investment advisers, economists, and financial analysts, will tell you retiring early is a terrible financial decision, many people have done it. Chris Reining retired at 37. Steve and Courtney Adcock did it at 35 and 33, and Grant Sabatier did it at 30, among other living examples.

Could you take a second and think about it? How daring and exciting would it be if you retired early?

e. It gives you a clear sense of direction.

Being led by the circumstance is the worst that can happen to anyone in retirement, and it is highly likely if you cannot foot your bills. When a person is led by circumstance, they cannot lay any plan for themselves. They just fold their arms across their chest by the window every day, wondering whether someone will kindly help them today. They cannot set a clear direction. They cannot choose when or where to travel because whoever provides for them is now in control. If they have no kids or relatives, they are limited by the peasant income they generate.

This may be a little too much for someone who has spent a large part of their life working so they'd have enough in their heydays as well as the last quarter of their lives. Smart investing is what gives you enough money to direct yourself upon retirement.

f. Happier marriage

In a 2021 study by the Jimenez law firm, it became apparent that "money arguments are the second leading cause of divorce, behind infidelity." In a broader picture, money is the primary reason couples depart besides infidelity. It holds a high profile that it is the first reason marriages break even when the teams are loyal. You don't have to wait until finances become a real problem in your marriage before building something sustainable.

g. Retirement does feel like retirement.

Retirement feels like retirement when you don't have to ride on a train among hundreds of commuters, sniffing several odors every morning. It feels like retirement when no one can threaten to cut your income for the month because you didn't show up at a given time or you did what you liked. In practical terms, retirement feels like retirement when you have enough money and time to go or do what pleases you.

h. Call the shots at retirement.

The unspoken reason most people stay under your command is that you give them money. If you can no longer offer it, you will likely lose your hold on them. You cannot command them to do things at your discretion, and they will hop on to the next person. It may sound cruel but most people seem loyal to you because they gain something in turn. When you can no longer offer it, they leave. On the flip side, you may need such people for political or personal reasons. To stay on top of such situations, you need enough money to call the shots.

i. Leave a legacy

We want to explore life and stay fulfilled, but our feeling is even more significant when we remember our altruistic desire to make life wonderful for the people who count on us. You might like to be a great dad, mom, or uncle for someone who looks bright and promising. You can teach good manners and impart honesty and other virtues. But one other thing you can leave behind is prosperity to ease the life adventures of your offspring. As American entrepreneur Jim Rohn described, "all good men and women must take responsibility to create legacies that will take the next generation to a level we could only imagine."

If there is a critical message from the preceding, you are likely to have a lot of debt, taxes, and ongoing bills at retirement. Whether or not you like it, post-retirement bills can get so high that your pension or 401(k) may not suffice.

This complex reality is what sometimes gets people kicked out of their own homes over debts. It also explains why many seniors sit across streets, holding out their hands for a dollar and struggling to live through the day despite being resplendent in their heydays. Now, you know why many houses are forfeited upon the demise of the original owner.

The crux is this - you may work hard, but you can quickly end up in these plights when you do not appropriately plan for your retirement. There is a big difference between current wealth and retirement wealth. Holding three jobs and generating tons of income from several sources in your prime does not guarantee wealth in retirement.

If you need to create a stable and secure income

at retirement, upping your retirement income game is a sine qua non. The brightest news at this point is that the magic formula for wealth at retirement is lying in the next chapter. Roll your sleeves and flip the page. Let's get down to business.

6

DON'T SAVE FOR RETIREMENT THE OLD WAY

Variety is the very spice of life that gives it its entire flavor. –
William Copper

I n the old days, people kept their money in the corner of the room. They dug holes and buried their valuables underground, and they sometimes handed the valuables to a local banker who kept things for everyone at a token. Today, we think we are significantly different. Yet, we do almost the same thing as most of us put our money in the bank, believing that we have preserved it.

In reality, we just do the same old things in a modern fashion. When you have some money to reserve, you open a checking or savings account and put the money there till the time you will need it. Banks usually charge a monthly maintenance fee to keep the account open, just like the traditional banker who charges a token to keep your resources.

While you think you are saving, the Forbes investor and activist Morgan Simon believes you are getting it wrong. In her words, "most people have been taught the virtues of saving for a rainy day. But want to hear something crazy? When you put your money in the bank nowadays, you usually LOSE money." This may not become immediately obvious because the bank returns precisely $100, the amount you saved with them when you call for it. Unfortunately, two things always happen, and neither is in your favor.

First, there is constantly raging inflation across the world. The United States Bureau of Labor Statistics says inflation is up by 7.5% from January 2021 to January 2022. This means if you had reserved $100 in January 2021, you would still have $100 in January 2022. But your $100 in 2022 is down by 7.5% in value. In essence, it can only afford what you needed $92.5 to purchase last year. So, your current $100 is not enough to buy what it could only last year. Strategically, you lost money. If you didn't lose $7 here and $25 there, you might not dig into your reserves to get cash for groceries, and you may have a bit more to prepare for retirement.

The second reality is that banks are constant investors. They pump money into several investment options and offer big loans to capitalists across the country. This is not bad. It is part of what they are set up to do. It is just that they are using your money, and you do not get a penny out of the interest they generate. Instead, they charge you for account maintenance.

These two realities will sting every businessperson who understands the value of money and the economy.

The full implication for anyone saving towards retirement is that using a typical savings account is a terrible choice. You are not only losing, but you are also giving money to those who will make their fortune from it.

The damaging reality is that this perspective is the most enforced across the United States. Society tells us that to be responsible citizens, we need to hold a stable job and make a steady income. Society goes even further, teaching us the misbelief that the best way to make a regular income is to spend most of our lives working for someone, following their rules, and exchanging our time — a resource we will never get back — for money. On top of that, we must save our money in the typical savings account, checking account, or piggy bank.

The proof is in a study published by the Statista Research Department in 2022. This study surveyed the various accounts owned by the children who participated. Up to 49% of them have a savings account; about 41% have a piggy bank. 9% have a PayPal account, 3% have a Venmo account, and up to 16% have none of these.

There are two disturbing figures in the entire study. Only 6% have an investment account, and 9% have a credit card. From all indications, society, by far, values debts, savings, and spending money more than investing.

When kids grow up with such mindsets, they are subconsciously conditioned to believe saving in a bank is gold. As we have seen, the reverse is the case. Therefore, the first demon you must fight in your attempt to guarantee financial prosperity at retirement is the urge to save money in the bank.

Grant Cardone, one of the intelligent people who retired early, actually believes that cash is trash. In his words, "you have the saying that cash is king.

But what if I told you it is not? Inflation eats it. $1000 in 1960 has the purchasing power of over $8000 today. That is why saving money is useless. Personally, I don't save money; I only store it for a short period until I can invest it."

We must draw a critical distinction at this point. Banks usually offer a wide variety of accounts, and some of them may serve as decent investment platforms with concrete terms and conditions. It is just that savings and checking accounts are the most popular, and the savings account is the traditional way to save.

Since you are constantly fighting inflation, you cannot let your money sit anywhere without generating significant profit. The first principle of generational wealth is that you must quit saving the old and unproductive way.

As Grant Cardone emphasizes, 'money needs to make babies to multiply," even if you save for a specific project such as buying a home, wedding, getting a car, et cetera, you must generate profits on it to guarantee some stability. I reckon you must be wearing the one million dollar question up your sleeve.

How then can you generate immense wealth while saving money?

a. Social investing is the answer.

The most practical answer is social investing. Banks take your money to invest in big business and make money for themselves. These big businesses already have things going for them. They make money from stocks and a large customer base and will not shut down without your funds. But little as it seems, your funds can make a significant part of small business investment.

On top of that, there are intelligent ways to invest such that you generate yields when you invest in a small business, and you can retain the value of your investment through profits, even in the face of staggering inflation.

In essence, the smart alternative is to put your money in a secure platform that generates yields rather than put your money in a traditional bank. CNote, Calvert Notes, and Media Development Notes are all savings options you can consider.

These saving options have a chosen specialty. It could be investing in businesses run by women or people of color, quick loans for small companies, et cetera, and their specialization is what they will pump your money into. Usually, they present you an annual interest rate (usually 2.5% or about while a traditional bank offers less than 1%), and your investment is insured. They also require you to keep the money with them for a specific period, after which you can request it. They may penalize you when you move the funds out earlier than the agreed "lock-up" period but that only teaches financial discipline.

Given that this system generates some profits even in the face of inflation, it is better than saving the traditional way.

b. Virtual banking

Alongside the first option, virtual banking is another innovative way to save money. In the observation of the financial analyst Mary Beth Eastman, "online banks generally offer lower rates, and they are sometimes free. They also provide a higher annual percentage yield (APY) on your savings than traditional banks. They are as insured as you ever need", suggesting that exploring them is an easy decision.

c. Pump it back in business

Grant Cardone would forever emphasize that money is not a mechanism to be reserved in any dormant wallet. It is an active catalyst that must make babies to remain valued. You need to make more money with your current money, and you can just pump it into an already established business. That could be yours or that of someone reliable with a track record of profit. You might think this sounds strikingly familiar since you invest in mutual funds, 401 (k) investments, et cetera. You are not wrong. Though there are better ways to do it, we will explore them across chapters 7, 8, and 9.

d. Purchase tangible assets that generate cash flow

Purchasing tangible assets that generate cash flow is one of the most innovative ways to reserve your money. In 2013, Jamie McDermont, a colleague, bought a house for about $267,000. He leased the place out and generated nearly $27000 annually. After four years, he sold the house off at $210000, walking away with over $40000 post-tax.

This is about 16% profit, a rate no savings account can generate within that period.

e. Saving in a foreign currency

If you have a high tolerance for risk, and you are happy to track the exchange rate, saving in foreign currencies may be the way to go for you. To start with, foreign currencies are generally volatile. Before you save in a foreign currency, you must understand that there is no permanence, and your national currency can grow in value against that currency. Similarly, your choice of foreign currency can rise against your national currency. If your money is saved in a different currency and your national currency rises against it, you might lose value on your money, and vice versa. Saving in another currency is wise only if you know how to track the exchange rate, and you can make moves before the market value dumps on your currency. People make an exceedingly huge profit from foreign exchange trading. They lose high too.

f. Do not rely so much on a savings account.

Consider creating funds for different purposes

rather than bank on your savings account as your absolute reserve. For instance, pump enough into your emergency funds. Financial experts often suggest that "enough" means your living expenses for six straight months. Similarly, create reserves for medical situations and fund your insurance. That way, you do not overly rely on a savings account.

The central idea behind this chapter is to help you block one of the well-known reasons the money you reserve does not amount to much. Already, we know that many people reserve money in their savings, and it is a habit developed in childhood. We understand that some people even reserve their retirement money in a savings account. If you are one such, you now understand that such practices achieve the exact opposite of what you hope to achieve. They now make you poorer.

g. Diversify

Yes, they were right. The investment advisors who told you to diversify your retirement investment have a valid point. Empirical studies reveal that businesses have varying success rates. Usually, those with low risks turn out low profits, and those with high risks turn out stupendous earnings if they work out - it is conditional. There are only a few cases where the investment risk and profit level are balanced.

As such, creating an investment portfolio becomes essential. Then, the portfolio should contain an array of investment options with different risk levels. According to the investment analyst Brian J. Block, "your age, risk appetite, and the size of your current assets is a determining factor when it comes to retirement investment risks." Anyone between 20 and 30 years can afford to make more risky investment choices. They can recoup if they run into heavy losses. They also have fewer responsibilities, so they can afford to crash if it does happen. People between 30 and 40 can withstand moderate risk. Anyone beyond such ages should be encouraged to take on steady, secure, and reliable investment options.

Now that this is rectified, let's hop on to the next chapter to discuss how to build slow, steady, reliable, and lifelong wealth for retirement.

7

BUILDING PASSIVE INCOME
THE 21ST CENTURY WAY

"Some people want it to happen, some wish it would happen, others make it happen" – Michael Jordan

The first and most reliable way to generate income at retirement is to build a passive income source. To be clear, a passive income is any source of generating money that requires little to no input from the profiting party.

According to a financial journalist at Bank Rate, James Royal, "passive income can come from rental property or a business in which one does not actively participate, such as being paid book royalties or stock dividends." From these three samples drawn by James Royal (book royalties, rental, and stock dividends), it is easy to see that passive income is about earning without being actively involved. It is a system where you just do something, then sit back, and earn life income.

Passive income does not include income from your job or your second job. Unless you are fully retired, your profit from your business cannot exactly be described as passive income either. Yes, you can indeed make money from your business as retired personnel who ventured into entrepreneurship upon retirement. It is possible to generate immense wealth from several other sources (which we will surely talk about), we just want to focus on passive income in this chapter.

There is no gainsaying this one. Passive income is the most secure way to thrive when you retire. It is an excellent way to receive monthly or annual income, just like your profit, and never worry about your bills because you always have enough to foot them. It is the most fulfilling way to earn money without actively working for it. Passive income is the most secure way to supplement your income and start actualizing items on your bucket list.

Please don't get it mixed up. Passive income is not a get-rich-overnight scheme. I must emphasize that it is not a way to harvest wealth that sprang out of the blues. You must do something. In fact, there are several activities to carry out before you can hope to earn through passive income. This chapter will explore the most reliable avenues that have generated income for millions and will continue for some time more, beginning from the most popular to the most obscure.

1. Real estate

Real estate is the most popular way to generate wealth in human history. The business has been relevant from the days of Mensa Musa to that of John D. Rockefeller and Andrew Carnegie, who opined that "ninety percent of all millionaires become so through owning real estate." Whether in college, in a bar, or down your street, you must have heard about real estate and its staggering potential.

To an average Jack, real estate is about buying a piece of land and building a shop or home for rent. When you tell someone you are into real estate, they instantly assume you have a piece of land for sale or a building you rake in rents from annually. While that is not off the point, many more activities are embedded in real estate. For instance, real estate includes leasing lands to factories, office spaces, and businesses like hotels and restaurants. It also comprises trading real estate in the stock exchange market and house flipping, among other advanced ventures. Beyond the typical methods of investing in real estate, some advanced strategies have flourished in the 21st century. There are ways to invest in real estate that require none of the old stress you used to go through, you don't have to own a particular property anymore. Without additional input, your real estate investment generates income for you every year. You don't even have to be the owner, and you can earn the income of an average American from the comfort of your room. Let's hop into the various ways you can invest in real estate and generate income now and continue long after retirement.

a. Crowdfunding

As the title suggests, crowdfunding is the art of raising funds from "a crowd" to sponsor a project. It is one of the ways business founders and managers get money to keep their businesses afloat. Due to the influx of tech, random persons who stumble upon the idea on a crowdfunding platform can also become investors.

Crowdfunding can be adopted in pretty much

any business, as you probably guessed. In typical cases, investors can earn an equity position in the enterprise, as in equity-based crowdfunding or they may get rewards and benefits such as participation in the launch of a new product or products being offered to them at a discounted price.

The advantage of crowdfunding as a tool for real estate investment is that it simplifies the process and makes it easy to invest in various properties. You indirectly own properties without going through the formalities, management stress, or paying mortgage like a traditional real estate investor.

In real estate, crowdfunding can be adapted for any purpose, starting from home buying to property flipping and REIG. There are four general ways to go about crowdfunding:

i. Donation-based crowdfunding

This is the least popular form of crowdfunding in real estate as people are persuaded to donate to a real estate project. Turnout is usually low in donation-based crowdfunding compared to the others. That is probably because the project manager offers nothing concrete in return to the people. Since you want to build lifelong wealth and generate profit on your investments, I do not see this as a wise option.

ii. Equity crowdfunding

Equity crowdfunding refers to a system where a business owner offers the potential investor an opportunity to own stakes in his company. This works more when a considerable amount is required to be raised for a project. It could also apply to other ventures asides from real estate, where the company has a viable product that can interest potential investors. It promises to generate huge revenues and it needs a sizable amount of money to get it off the ground.

To ensure the investors are wholly committed, a founder might offer them a measured percentage of the company's ownership. It is a good option for someone looking to build a lifelong income because it allows one to own a part of the company's profits irrespective of the level of active participation. Profits and yields are shared according to the investment ratio, but one big con is that if things go down south, creditors will be paid before investors, who are equity partners.

iii. Reward-based crowdfunding

Reward-based crowdfunding is the non-committal system where a business manager is only looking to people who will collaborate to actualize the product the company is working on. The investors have no shares in the company; they are only entitled to certain benefits. For instance, they can share in the profit. They may also be eligible to receive the first delivery or products at a significantly subsidized rate. This system is commonly used in new technologies/software creation, or even scientific research.

iv. Debt Crowdfunding

Debt crowdfunding is another popular option in the real estate crowdfunding market. The idea here is to meet people who are not interested in staking anything in the project. They are not interested in equity or rewards. All they want is an interest you must not default on. If the project yields a more significant income than was estimated, they have no right to request more. They also have to be paid if much smaller profits were made than initially estimated.

There are two parties in all of these; the partner who raised the crowdfunding and the investors. As someone looking to build a permanent income, your role should be an investor. This means you will not participate in the operation or execution of the project. You just put your money and expect agreed yields.

It is not so easy, either. You have to watch out for specific traits so you don't lose your investment. For instance, you need to ensure that the fund management team has a track record of success. It would help if you were sure that the executives were competent enough to carry out the project through education and practice. It would be best if you also verified the legitimacy of the entire enterprise. It doesn't end there; ensure that you have an average of 11% to 15% return every year, regardless of the circumstance. So, from the start, there is a lot of homework to do. This is higher than the average 7-10% yield in a 401 (k) or 403 (b), making it a better option, though riskier.

In some cases, you are required to be an accredited investor, meaning that you earn at least $200,000 annually or are worth well over a million dollars to be eligible. You should expect to pay taxes on income generated from this. Depending on the package, you can earn this profit for as long as the agreement stands. So, as you near your retirement, it is wise to have a lot of guaranteed real estate crowdfunding projects in a long-term affiliation. It is also intelligent to back this with equity crowd-funding. Without working at all, you can earn forever. While you can start with only a few hundred dollars in some situations, you may also pump as much as possible (based on a track record of success) since your profit is proportionate to your investment.

All thanks to technology, you can easily pick a real estate crowdfunding project to invest in. You only need to sign up on a real estate crowdfunding website and select a project. Crowdfunding plat-forms with high reputation include Fundrise, Peer-Street, YieldStreet, RealtyMogul, Crowdstreet, EquityMultiple, and Diversify fund. Review the websites; compare their services, fee structures, weak points, and loopholes before investing.

More importantly, consider their requirements and evaluate which one provides investment options that match your preferred type of investment (equity, loan, et cetera.) Remember to consult your accountant to determine the tax implication of each investment option in your state or country, and also review the feedback of people who have invested in each platform. If you can go through this homework, you can guarantee a safe and high-quality retirement source of income that can go into forever.

b. House flipping

Next to crowdfunding, house flipping is another popular way to generate income in real estate. The truth about house flipping is that it is not a passive means of payment. Instead, it requires evaluation, professional overview, property valuation, strategic estimations, and lots more. You found it here because even though it is not exactly a passive source, it can generate income for you in the long run.

Whether you have a background here or not, you can start a house flipping with proceeds of your pension or 401k upon retirement. What you need are some tiny yet vital clips I will discuss now.

As described by the finance and real estate journalist James Mcwhiney, "house flipping is a real estate investing strategy in which an investor purchases a property not to use, but with the intention of selling it for a profit." Your most important job is to buy a property (or a group of properties), touch it up, and sell it at standard value.

As straightforward as the job sounds, it requires some expertise, and it is easy to flop since it is all based on estimations. First, you need professional appraisal services to value the house and estimate its After-repair value (ARV). The next step is to sum up the cost of acquiring the property with the cost of repairs, which must include the charge of professionals involved in the process. As a rule of thumb, the total expenses incurred on buying and renovating the property must be no more than 70% of its standard value when it is ready for sale (ARV). This is the one way to guarantee that you make some profit at the end of the day, no matter what.

It sounds like a good business for a retiree since you will not involve in any strenuous activity. The stats also proved that the business thrives across the States. Over 245,800 houses were flipped in the United States in 2019. It is essential to hire a professional appraisal team to estimate what it would take to fix the house and its standard value upon repairs. That way, you can tell whether this will be a good buy.

Unlike the crowdfunding system where you are not actively involved in the entire process, house flipping requires you to study the property and its potential. If you do not wish to hang around your home every day and night upon retirement, a business like this can keep you busy. Unlike the crowd-funding system where you are guaranteed income annually/ monthly (depending on the arrangement,) house flipping does not offer you instant yields.

First, you must spend months finding a good house. Then, take some time to fix it up, and take weeks to months to get a buyer. Nevertheless, you can make more than enough to foot your bills by flipping only one or two properties in a year. Assuming that you bought a property worth $300,000 ARV, in the practical sense, if you sell at the after-repair value, you will pocket 30%, being $90,000 from the single sale. You may even sell the property at a price higher than the ARV, and you can flip several properties annually. Maybe I don't have to say this, but whether you delve into flipping houses before or during retirement, the proceeds are sufficient to keep your bills well under control when you retire.

There are a few cautions, though. Your success in this industry depends on how much cash you have to purchase. Remember that beyond purchasing, you still need funds for repairs. You also have to be sure you hire suitable personnel. Alongside, you need not sell too early or too late. This business requires a lot of patience, money, and smartness. While you may enjoy it in your old age, it is more fun to take risks while younger. Do it a few times and make profits while you are still active at work - if you are going to do it at all.

c. Buy and hold

Buy and hold is another popular way to invest in real estate. As described by the sensational real estate investor Konrad Soipelinikow, "buy and hold in real estate is a long-term investment strategy where an investor purchases a property and holds on to it for an extended period." Generally, buy-and-hold is an investment system used to describe the tact of purchasing an investment bloc and reserving it for a long time when its value must have shot up.

In the real estate scenario, the investment bloc might be a piece of land, a residential home, an office space, a vacation home, et cetera. The central idea is to purchase one such property until a few years when it would presumably generate more value. You may lease out the property to generate income during the waiting period.

Unlike most other investment options, buy and hold protects your money against inflation since real estate typically appreciates with inflation. It offers a sizeable return on investment compared to most other options. For instance, you can get over 200% yield in 10 years. It also generates annual or monthly income that can foot some of your bills. You must brace up because you cannot quickly sell off such properties should you urgently need cash.

Across the United States, people who buy and hold properties generally get tax benefits, mortgage interest deduction, exemption from FICA taxes of social security, et cetera.

Before purchasing a property like this, you must ensure that the monthly income that can be gener-ated from it can pay off your monthly expenses. You should sign up for courses on analyzing future trends, population data, neighborhood prospects, et cetera. You should also consider making a down payment of up to 25% of the cost of purchase and drawing a loan on the rest. I don't have to remind you that the property's potential value is a vital figure you should consider before getting such property.

You can expect significant long-term profits if you own a buy-and-hold property. At the same time, you must prepare for debts, insurance, tenant troubles, and property management. This is one of the tricky businesses that blend active with passive income. The bulk of the work is to get the property. Upon purchase, profits are in the coffers, but you must manage the property right or hire a property manager, which means additional costs.

Before and upon retirement, getting a buy-and-hold property is brilliant. You can purchase one in your 30s, 40s, or even 50s. You may equally buy one with your retirement pension- if it is given as a one-time lump sum. While it is not necessary, getting a mentor can quicken your success pace in the industry. Some promising cities in the United States for buy-and-hold investors include Nashville, TN, Jacksonville, FL, Pittsburgh, PA, Hunstville, AL, Houston, TX, Cleveland, OH, Orlando, FL, Chicago, IL, Indianapolis, IN, and Tampa, FL. These cities have higher prospects because of factors such as greater demand for rental properties, higher rental income, low tenant default rate, steady population and job growth, and rising home prices. These factors are applicable across different countries in deciding where to purchase a buy-and-hold investment.

d. Real estate shares

Do you recall the equity crowdfunding system?

Right, it is the art of getting people to fund a real estate project in return for equity. The distinguishing fact about the crowdfunding system is that technology facilitates it. You don't have to know the founder or participate in the management process. You evaluate the stats and fund the project.

Similarly, some real estate options allow you to invest and get shares without getting actively involved in any property management. We will discuss them in the following few lines.

Real Estate Investment Trust (REIT)

As stated by one of the foremost REIT companies, NAREIT, "a real estate investment trust is a finance company specializing in investing and generating income from a range of property sectors." Basically, a REIT owns, operates, or finances real estate projects and generates income for all parties. A REIT is usually publicity traded.

Like mutual funds and crowdfunding, a REIT gathers capital from several investors and then invests in a range of properties and real estate options. Investment choices may range from hotels to data centers, healthcare, cell towers, office buildings, and retail stores, to mention a few. Usually, REITs focus on commercial properties (over residential properties). The Internal Revenue Code requires a REIT to invest 75% of its total assets in real estate.

As mentioned earlier, REITs are mostly publicly traded in the stock market. However, private REITs do not register with the Security Exchange Commission, which means their shares are only available to private entities. To use the words of the real estate investor James Chen, "REITs are easy to buy and sell as most trade on public exchanges."

In a case where REIT is publicly traded, you can purchase stocks through a broker. You may also purchase through private entities if you match their investment requirements, and you are certain that your funds will be insured. As an investor, you are not required to take part in property management, and the law is that 90% of all REIT profit should be shared with investors as dividends. This makes it an ideal source of "pension" for a retiree, but you should know that the progress rate is generally low since profit is always shared, and the business is subject to high market risks.

A new Morningstar Associates analysis, sponsored by Nareit, found that the optimal portfolio allocation to REITs ranges between 4% and 13%. While this doesn't sound bad, you might like to know that the investment expert, Matthew DiLallo examined the performance of the REITs versus the S&P 500 from 1972 to 2019 and found that while S&P 500 had a total annual return of 12.1%, that of REITs overall was 13.3%. Although S&P 500 outperformed REITs in 2019 and the previous 10-year period, data over the long term has set REITs ahead. Some REITs subgroups have even outperformed the S&P 500 over the last 10-year period such as self-storage REITs and the leading Industrial REIT Prologis.

In essence, REITs outperformed the S&P 500 steadily, and people should look to divert a part of their retirement allocation to it.

To invest in REIT, you need to pick a few REITs and review their range of investments. Evaluate the investments to guesstimate their dividend yield and the prospect of growth in the industry. The gearing ratio is another critical factor to consider. The gearing ratio is the ratio of debt to owned assets. A high gearing ratio indicates that the REIT is in a lot of debt and will likely generate less profit. You also need to review its share price. While REIT seems straightforward, it is ideal to get a mentor with vast experience and expertise so you can have early access to industry facts that newbies learn the hard way. With this out of the way, REIT is a safe way to generate lifelong wealth upon retirement.

Real Estate Investment Group (REIG)

REIG is a great avenue to generate wealth for enthusiasts in the real estate industry. As the real estate investor Liz Brummer Smith describes REIG, "it is a group of private investors who invest primarily in real estate by pooling money, knowledge, or time to acquire properties that generate income." So, it is a system where people put their money, time, and expertise together to make money together in real estate.

The general picture is this - a Real Estate Investment Group is formed. The group builds or purchases some properties, and then sells them in units to investors who must be group members. The property is then leased out to the public and managed by the group. In turn, the group charges a fixed percentage as management commission, and the bulk of the rent goes to the investors according to the number of units they own.

You must remember this - REIG varies according to each organization and state policies. Sometimes, you are required to offer some expertise to be a part of the group. If you do not possess this expertise, you may choose either to back out or to explore possible options for non-professionals and seniors.

Investing in REIG is straightforward. You do not require a lot of time since the group manages and repairs the properties in most cases. You however need to find a team of experienced professionals who are also trustworthy people. The National Real Estate Investors Association (REIA) is an excellent resource for local REIG groups. You can also search on platforms like LinkedIn, Craigslist, local communities' websites, et cetera.

As a rule of thumb, it is not wise to invest in the business if it offers a limited partnership because that implies that it is set up to make a profit for a few years and shut down afterward. Remember that this is for your retirement; you need something that can generate profit long after you stop active work.

Real Estate ETF/Mutual Fund

The preliminary step to understanding real estate ETF is to know how ETF works. ETF is an acronym for Exchange Traded Funds and they are traded directly on the exchange market. The investment author Kevin Vogt explains, "ETFs are traded in the stock market in the standard trading hours, and have tickers, just like stocks." The key difference is that ETFs focus on index funds. For instance, an ETF might trade in gold, electric vehicles, Nasdaq composite, et cetera.

An ETF can also allow you to diversify your portfolio by buying several securities with your single investment. It is precisely how mutual funds work except for the fact that you can trade mutual funds after the market closes while ETF works during normal trading hours. Besides that, you can buy on a margin, and stop and limit orders with an ETF, but you can only add or remove your capital with mutual funds.

From the foregoing, it is easy to tell that a real estate ETF focuses on real estate commodities and agencies. Like a typical real estate fund, it allows you to invest in several opportunities rather than stick to only one high-performing REIT. Essentially, you are investing in REITs strategically, which will enable you to invest in several funds with a single investment. Vanguard Real Estate Index Fund, Schwab US REIT ETF, SPDR Fund, and iShares Cohen & Steers REIT ETF are among the highest performing REIT ETFs in the United States. Similarly, you may consider mutual funds like the Neuberger Berman Real Estate Fund, Cohen & Steers Intl Realty Shares, Guggenheim Risk Managed Real Estate Fund, Baron Real Estate Fund, et cetera.

The significant advantage of ETF and Mutual funds is that you can trade them at leisure. You can buy and sell anytime. You can also trade them online. You should know that there is always a risk of loss which can make it an unreliable source of income.

e. Rental property

In plain English, rental property is any property you own to lease out over time. Buy-and-hold properties, which we have earlier discussed, are perfect examples, but unlike them, a typical rental property is held for rental purposes. You may hold rental properties for short or long terms. This is where the terms Long-Term Rentals (LTR) and Short-Term Rentals (STR) originate.

As the name implies, a long-term rental is one such property you lease out for an extended period, anything between one year and twenty. This is common in commercial properties like factories, office spaces, a piece of land, et cetera. On the flip side, a short-term rental refers to a property leased out for a brief moment, as little as a few hours, days, weeks, or a couple of months at the max. A system like that is popular with hotels, vacation homes, Airbnb, Vrbo, Golightly, et cetera.

House hacking is another concept directly related to rental properties. Victoria Araj, a real estate content critic, describes it as "the art of finding ways to generate income from your home. It is about buying multi-family properties, living in a unit, and renting out the others so that the tenants can pay the owner's mortgage, or generate more income for the owner".

Owning a rental property is arguably the most considered option among retirees of all real estate investment strategies. According to Emily Brandon in a 2018 report by the U.S. News and World Report, "the number of renters in their early 60s increased by 84 percent between 2006 and 2016." Also, one in eight homeowners aged 65 to 74 years made an own-to-rent transition over the decade. This means they switched from becoming complete owners to leasing some part of the house. This is partly to reduce the maintenance stress and generate income.

Whether you consider the STR or LTR, there are legitimate reasons rental properties are wonderful sources of revenue for you upon retirement. "Unlike the traditional ways to retire," Jeff Rohde, a real estate manager, explains, "rental properties provide steady cash flow, reliable appreciation, leverage, tax benefits, among other options." The British Member of Parliament, John Stuart Mill, certainly knows what he implies by "landlords grow rich in their sleep."

You must know that rental properties are not entirely passive. You have to manage the property, handle repairs, and prepare to deal with tenants. Should you desire to refrain from active management, you must consider getting a property manager, which cuts from your profits but leaves you completely free. Before deciding on a rental option to explore, you must consider one fundamental question.

How much would you need in retirement?

There is no one way to look at it. As we have earlier said, it is all about your estimates. If you estimate that you will need about $60,000 annually, for instance, then you will need a property that generates up to $5,000 monthly. According to the Business Insider report on the American Community Survey from 2017, "the highest median rent in this U.S. is in Hawaii with $1507 a month. The least is in South Dakota with $696 per month." This places the U.S. average at $1249, which Carolyn Morris, a finance and audiobook expert, suggests.

At $1249 a month on each home, you need at least four homes to meet your $5000 goal. Couple this with the fact that you must put some amount away in reserve for repairs, property management, insurance, and tax, and you will realize you need up to 7 homes. This is precisely what the real estate manager Jeff Rohde suggests for a $60000 annual income, and that is if you are free of mortgage debt.

"Whoa! No way"

"Phew! How is anyone going to own seven homes? You are kidding?"

In an instant, the pictures of seven homes might flash in your head and appear vague because it seems pretty tough to imagine yourself owning up to that. What if you need more than $60,000? Would you have to own more homes?

The answer is no. The first fact is that our estimate was based on the average residential rent. If you are tactical about this, you can invest in high-yielding environments where you can get up to $1500 or more on each home. Over the last ten years, the real estate industry has consistently seen an average increase year on year in the rate of rents. These past trends, coupled with insider analysis, give the real estate analyst and reporter, Ben Winck, the impression that "rents will keep going up. The median apartment rent in the U.S. has gone up by about 9.2%, and new data suggests that rent prices will keep climbing at a breakneck pace."

This leaves a massive clue for you; next year offers more promises than the current year. With a system like this, things can only get better for anyone heavily living on it.

Besides, these estimations are based on Long Term Rentals. If you try house hacking by building or purchasing multi-family homes, you can seamlessly generate your needs from only three properties rather than five. You can also consider some Short Term Rentals.

Generally, LTR provides a more stable and predictable income each year. As long as there are no upsets and accidents, you can easily estimate how much you would make each year. But STRs are not so stable. They are mostly seasonal since such homes are built for vacations, short-term hosting, and tourist purposes. Ironically, empirical studies reveal that an STR generates a significantly higher income during an active season than an LTR all year.

With an LTR, you may get stuck with a tenant who causes trouble. Your tenants have rental rights as dictated by the state, and you have a process to go through before evicting them. On the other side of the coin, STR tenants are temporary. They usually pay upfront, and the chances of damages are minor. You can also charge any significant damage to their credit card.

If you are going for an LTR, you can passively manage it. You can easily get loans or mortgages for another property, and you are not excessively constricted by state or house owner association policies in your community. You can also slash the utility costs and maintenance charges with the tenants.

For an STR, you may face trouble when you meet an underwriter to access your ability to take on new loans. You only stand a chance if you have raked in an average income for five years or about on your STR. Similarly, you cannot transfer your bills to your tenants. You also need to locate your STR around tourist centers, resort towns, beach or skiing communities, et cetera.

The central idea is that there are pros and cons on each side of rental properties. If you enjoy vacations and you may be looking to go often, it is ideal to own an STR. With virtual platforms like Airbnb and Vrbo, getting clients who match your price is super easy. While it is possible to manage STR upon retirement, it can prove more stressful than an LTR, and you may be drawn away from home often. Again, the essence of retirement is lost unless that is what you want to spend your retirement doing.

However, if you are more conservative and think you can manage a few tenants, you are better off with LTR. When you invest in suitable properties and scrutinize your tenants before hiring them, you have a huge chance of having fewer troubles than the average. Consider taking a course on LTR or STR investing.

2. Online Education

Right after Real Estate, Online Education is the next most extensive way to guarantee steady income upon retirement. As the encyclopedia defines it, "online education is a flexible instructional delivery system that encompasses any kind of learning that takes place via the internet." You engage in it when you sign up for classes and courses, attend seminars, or take part in other educational activities on the internet.

In a Statista report by the author and education enthusiast, Erin Duffin, he stated that "up to 63% of U.S. high school students use e-learning tools every day. Elementary, Middle School, and College students also use the online system." If the statistics mean nothing to you, pause to reflect on the fact that there are over 15 million high school students, and up to 63% of them use e-learning facilities every day. The matter of contention is this - with the massive adoption of online education, you can generate lifelong wealth and a steady retirement income through online education. We will talk about the various ways to do it now.

i. Teach in a system

The first and most realistic way to profit from the massive adoption of online education is to teach in a system. This means you should sign up on an online platform that allows you to teach something you are extremely good at and others want to know. By way of illustration, you may choose to teach the English language to international students who adopt it as a second or foreign language (TESL or TEFL.) In such situations, you are often (not always) required to have a degree or a TEFL/TESOL certificate. There are online institutions you can also enroll in to obtain such certificates. You should have no trouble with this if you are a native English language speaker unless you're not.)

Before you wipe that off your mind, you need to know that you do not have to teach English in a system. Many educational platforms only require you to have proven expertise and a certificate you probably got during your active years of service. By way of illustration, an accountant with an accounting degree is almost qualified to teach accounting. The online platform (especially if it is not a typical school) can enroll you in a teaching course just before you are admitted as an active teacher on their platform. Similarly, you can teach programming, SEO (search engine optimization), data analysis, cooking, business management, podcasting, public speaking, finance and budgeting, et cetera.

You can teach your area of specialization or a side skill you have and the world needs. Think about soft skills like conflict management, negotiation skills, human relations, et cetera. There are loads of knowledge you have learned on your job. You just need to decide on one and bank on the fact that you have seen enough of it to understand what it is all about. You need to do some reading and research, but ultimately, pick a subject in which your years in practice will provide you with an edge over others.

So that you know, this system may not extensively foot your expenses. The famous job recruiting agency in the United States, Zip Recruiter, suggests that "about $19 per hour is the average earning for an online teacher across the United States." This grosses about $3000 a month. It gets smaller with taxes, and it may not match your retirement expenses. However, it is a seamless way to get students and teach the unspoken facts you learned the hard way to less experienced people.

It is an exciting way to spend your time and help people learn from your experience. It is also a good option for retirement since you will work online most time, and you can decide when or when not to work. On top of that, you may settle into a comfortable retirement if you have additional income from pension, rental properties, or REIT.

Check out Simplilearn, Edureka, Upgrad, Teachable, and so forth to sign up as a teacher. Considering that this is tech-oriented and these platforms may not entirely serve your specialization, it is best to hop online and punch "best platform to teach [your preferred skill] online." The search results are all yours to devour.

ii. Set up your system

Setting your system up is the broadest way to generate profit in the online education system. As the title suggests, setting up your system implies that you completely control your education system. You determine the medium through which the students learn or how to make profits. You are also not limited to any platform's policies or payment patterns.

The first system you can easily set up is a blog. The editorial staff at WpBeginner believes that "a blog is a type of website where the content is presented in a reverse chronological order, and it serves as an online diary." You can take a blog as a website where you can publish what would originally be in your diary. Be specific on a particular niche this time because you can have readers worldwide. A typical blog contains details, content, facts, figures, and other relevant information in your selected space.

If you choose politics as your niche, you must frequently update political stories on your blog. You should talk about political parties, social statistics, politics, policies, et cetera. If you are in the culinary niche, the subjects of discussion on your blog will border around food, skills, and arts.

Again, you must boast industry experience in any niche you address. This makes it relatively easy for you to fill up the blog with expensive content despite your age and you will not need to engage in aggressive learning as such. For instance, if you have been a water engineer, you are one of the most qualified to discuss pertinent topics. If you have worked as a chef for the past 30+ years, you can seamlessly create topics and high-quality content on commercial cookery. This applies to someone who has been a freelancer, business leader, startup manager, secretary, relationship counselor, et cetera.

According to the famous email management system, OptinMonster, "77% of internet users worldwide like reading blogs." An approximate 403 million users read blog stories every month. This figure promises to go higher because more people continue to adopt the internet. A similar study by OptinMonster affirms that people read blog stories more than their emails. Going by the rate of internet adoption in recent times, it is easier to find readers who would be willing to read your content, learn a great deal and even go on to subscribe to your platform. This means you may offer a subscription-based blog where one has to pay to read articles like Medium.com, Copyblogger, BBC Muzzy, and so forth.

If creating written content may be tedious, consider switching to podcasts or videos. Through platforms like Audible and YouTube, you can create audio and video content that customers may need to pay for before accessing. The amount you make on this largely depends on the number of your subscribers and the number of views generated. So, you need a digital marketer to help you push your product in the face of those who genuinely need them.

Besides the subscription model, you can sell other people's products as an affiliate. You may not directly charge your audience any amount when accessing your content. Instead, you can profit from the commissions you get when your audience purchase affiliate products through your link. I will explain this when we extensively discuss affiliate marketing.

Again, you can start as an actual teacher. You can choose to be an 'edprenuer', set up your platform, and market yourself. You can do this by setting up a course on a website where you teach people. You can equally use platforms like Udemy and LinkedIn.

Many Yoga teachers, business management executives, and human resource managers do this. Already, life has garnished you with the required experience. You only need to embellish it with a bit of research to keep abreast with new developments in your field. Empirical studies reveal that on average, teachers with their platforms earn about $1-5k each month. People like Dave Fox, Brendan Jackson, Deborah Nieman, and Guy Windsor comfortably sit around $10-50k every month. Maybe that changes your mind on the whole.

Getting started is simple. You need to review other courses to see what people complain about. See areas learners want to understand, but most teachers skip. Go through social media posts, see what people genuinely need help with, and see which you can solve. Consider taking a course on setting up a successful virtual teaching career or sign up for mentorship with those who have done it.

3. Becoming an author

This is another substantial means to generate income on the internet. There are tons of subjects you can write books on, and you can be sure that there are avid readers across the world. For instance, in the United States, over 60% read at least five books a year. You only have to remember that the United States boasts of over 300 million people to appreciate the large number of books being consumed.

You bought this book to learn about building retirement income, likewise, people buy to learn other things. There is certainly a thing or two that you know and can author a book on. If you deal with a publisher, there is no telling how much you can passively earn in royalties.

There is also the option of exploring self-publishing. As reported by Amazon's 2019 review of Kindle sales, self-published authors earn as high as over $50,000 annually from their book sales. This applies to the fiction and non-fiction niches. Several self-publishing groups offer in-depth coaching on how to excel in this field. You can consider signing up with any of them.

Interestingly, you need not wait till retirement to start exploring these options. You can start today. Fail, when necessary, and comfortably build a business you can constantly generate revenue streams from in the future.

4. Debt Investment

According to Sharestates, an investment agency, "debt investment refers to an investor lending money to a firm or project sponsor with the expectation of the borrower paying back the investment with interest."

Technically, you purchase a debt (you lend them or clear their debt) from a company believing that they will pay it back with interest. If you recall, this sounds like debt crowdfunding, a system where you are not interested in the yields of the real estate project but only want your interests.

A debt may be secured or unsecured. It is secure when the creditor is offered a surety that can be sold should the debtor refuse to pay. Assets that may be used as surety include real estate property, car, gold, bonds (which is also a debt), deposits, et cetera.

On the flip side, unsecured loans are issued based on the borrower's creditworthiness. The nearest example is a credit card loan. Other examples are loans taken on by large corporations, capital projects, and the government.

If you do not know, the government has always obtained debts from the citizens through specific systems. The National Priorities Project reports that "to finance the federal debt, the U.S. Treasury sells bonds and other types of 'securities' which anyone can buy." So, by buying bonds and treasury securities, you have loaned money to the government.

Before making any debt investment, it is crucial to consider the type of firm you are choosing to invest in, where the debt was generated, the purpose of selling the debt, and the investment returns it offers.

Bonds, loans, and treasury securities are ideal choices for you only if you have other promising sectors to invest in, but you wish to include a few reliable supplements. The returns are diminutive to consider them your sole retirement investment. So, look to adding other investment platforms that can generate recurrent yield.

5. Affiliate Marketing

In the direct explanation of the Investopedia investment analyst, Jake Frankenfield, "Affiliate marketing is an advertising model in which a company compensates third-party publishers to generate traffic or leads to the company's products and services." To do this, the company creates an affiliate system that encourages professional affiliates to partner with the company, generate leads (potential customers), and get a commission fee from every purchase made by the customers.

The best way to grasp the picture is to put yourself in it. Imagine you are an affiliate, and Company B is offering you a 30% commission for every successful purchase you make (the typical affiliate commission is 20-30%). So, each time you bring a customer who purchases the company's product worth $1000, you are entitled to $300. You don't have to go about the street finding customers who would buy the products. Instead, you will need a loyal audience who uses pertinent products. For instance, if you are going to affiliate with an e-Bike company, your customers must be average Tom and Harry, who likely work in distant places and might have use for the bike.

Do you affiliate with a Yoga or body fitness company? Then, you need to have an audience of youths and adults who worry about physical or mental wellness. This means you must have niched around mental care at work, body fitness for self-confidence, et cetera. When you create several helpful pieces of content, your audience will come to trust you and will purchase whatever you sell as an affiliate. Remember, you will buy a Bible your pastor recommends. You will pay for a textbook your favorite professor emphasizes. You will also watch a YouTube Channel or buy a kit recommended by your basketball coach. It makes perfect sense that your blog readers, podcast listeners, or vlog viewers are naturally inclined to purchase whatever you recommend when they trust your brand. This way, a hundred persons, a thousand, or even more can purchase a product for which you get $300 per person without fuss. At the same time, you must verify the quality of the product or service, so your reputation is not smeared.

The most exciting fact is that you do not have to go outside your boundary to create content or get affiliate proposals. You can create content around niches you find comfortable, whether health care and mental wellness or business and professional development. Afterward, you can get affiliates for products directly related to your content.

You can do this at any age as long as you have no health complications that hamper you from talking on a podcast or Youtube. You need to constantly offer value and deal only with companies with high integrity. You can join affiliate platforms like Clickbank, Amazon affiliate, Fiverr, Bluehost, Hostinger, Shopify, Ali Dropship, Weebly, et cetera. You can also work with small businesses.

6. Multi-Level Marketing.

Are you the outgoing person who brings life to every room the instant you're in? If yes, multi-level marketing is an excellent choice of passive income for you. But if you're not, you still can learn if you are keen on a career in multi-level marketing.

What is it all about?

In the words of the investment analyst, Evan Tarver, "The term multi-level marketing (MLM) refers to a strategy used by some direct sales companies to sell products and services. MLM encourages existing members to promote and sell their offerings to other individuals and bring recruits into the business. Distributors are paid a percentage of their recruits' sales."

In other words, it is a system of selling products that banks on interpersonal communication and selling directly to people in exchange for a commission on every sale. Here, billboards, social media, or T.V. advertisements are not the focus, instead, network marketing is used. Simultaneously, other people are encouraged to join the system and sell products. A chain of traders and the people they have recruited is subsequently formed such that a percentage of money is paid to each individual based on the number of recruits connected to them and their corresponding sales.

It is similar to a pyramid, except that this is more realistic. Many MLM systems are also shady and illegal and have ripped people of their hard-earned money. So, if you are going to engage in an MLM, you need to research and verify that it is entirely legal in your country. Examples of legally established MLMs are Avon, Amway, and Herbalife nutrition. They all operate in several countries.

The significant advantage of MLM is that you don't have to work forever. Your most important job is to sell to a few people and bring in recruits. You will earn commission as long as your recruits continue to bring sales and recruits. They will gain from their recruits, and you will make profits too. The more recruits you get, the higher your profits at the end of each month.

You must understand that MLMs are dicey. You often have to work hard and bring in a lot of recruits while selling several products before you can hope to sit back and earn income from the system. This means a lot of convincing, sales, and networking are required. If you are not up for something so demanding, you may have to look at the other options we have discussed.

Over and above, passive income is realistic upon retirement. There are many ways to generate income when you're no longer active in the workplace. Some may require a little effort, and a lot (like blogging) blend into an excellent way to retire. I must tell you that this list is by no means exhaustive. I bobbed several businesses out because they have less potential or may be more stressful. I recommend these businesses more than others, and I have seen several people build stable retirement with them.

Interestingly, there are a few other semi-passive sources to generate wealth income which we shall discuss in the final chapter of this book. Before going on to that, shall we talk about pertinent ways of cutting costs as a retiree?

8

CUTTING COSTS AS A RETIREE

These days, you've gotta milk a dollar out of every dime –
Gayle Forman

You will have several bills and several sources of income. We have made this much clearer from the start of this guide. Conversely, this chapter chooses to approach retirement from an entirely different perspective. While you worry about footing your retirement bills, why don't you look at practical ways to cut your expenses?

If you can cut down your expenses as a retiree, you will require smaller amounts to live on each month. You will have less worry about footing bills and have enough time to go about the most important things to you at that moment. If you need medication, vacation, or visitation to people around you, you can easily do all of it with enough bills off your worries.

This underscores the essence of cutting costs as a retiree. It also makes it easier to meet your financial requirements when you are no longer active at work. From all indications, cutting costs is vital for every intending retiree.

How then can you cut costs?

a. Have no debts

According to retirement expert, Rodney A. Brooks, "having no debt is one of the most effective ways to cut your costs upon retirement." With no mortgage, credit card, or auto loans, navigating your monthly bills is easier since it is around groceries and utilities. With almost no debts, many people can moderately live on their pension or social security (depending on the general cost of living around them.)

Even if your pension does not cover your entire expenses, you have only a little behind, and you can protect that from returns in any other retirement venture. Having no debts also implies that you own equity over your property. You are also not at risk of eviction or drastic actions by credit companies.

Excess pressure can lead to several health conditions in a retired person. This is the primary reason a retiree should not face financial hurdles, especially from credit card companies, mortgages, or auto loans. It is not just the corporate entities, try to clear your debts with friends and relatives as early as possible. Sometimes, such steps may require you to put up a car for sale or sell a property or some other asset. Still, it is better to clear debts than hold on to properties you may not overly need.

b. Avoid overwhelming commitments

To directly adopt the words of the American author and business consultant, Ken Blanchard, "there is a difference between interest and commitment. When you are interested in doing something, you do it only when it is convenient. When you are committed to something, you accept no excuses, only results." The implication for you is that you may put yourself in overwhelming financial trouble by making commitments.

You may have made commitments to organizations, memberships, and platforms where your financial contribution is mandatory. While they may be generally beneficial, many of these platforms eat away your retirement income and surge your retirement bills. You have more bills to pay, and you do not get a significant increase in value, though you may feel personal satisfaction. Let's face it. Such expenses are luxury, and you cannot afford them if you feel their effects on your finances. It is best to trim them off.

c. House hacking

House hacking is another strategic way to cut down your monthly expenses. First, the cost of energy, garden maintenance, water bills, and other bills can be split when you are not the only resident. It is even more straightforward when you bring in a roommate. You can split the energy bills and several other utilities. While you should not expect it, a younger roommate can offer to foot a large percentage of the accounts while lightening your bills further.

Beyond the fact that house hacking enables you to share your bills, it increases your income which means you have more money and fewer expenses. It is a no-brainer.

d. Trimming your bucket list

This is something nobody tells you, but you have to accept it here and now. Dreams are wonderful, but they don't always come to pass. Many things on your bucket list may not be realistic, and you have to come to terms with that.

Unless you have enough funds to foot the bills, traveling across 50 countries is one of the expensive items that you can delete from your bucket list. You are now a grown-up. You know what you are capable of and what you might struggle to accomplish. There is no general way to fathom what could be seamless to accomplish and what money can impede.

e. Retire in a less expensive environment

"When you are trying to balance a fixed income with an enjoyable retirement, the cost of living is a crucial factor to consider," says the investment advisor, Stacy Rapacon. Tough as it may sound, selling off your home to purchase one in an environment where your cost of living is reduced is an intelligent way to improve your finances. Suppose you move to a country like Ecuador, where $1,650 to $1,825 can conveniently get a couple through each month, then your pension or social security will be sufficient to foot your bills, compared to what you may experience if you have to stay back in a U.S. city where you need a minimum of $4500 to live through the month.

To avoid having a large house and incurring high maintenance bills, people often suggest that you downsize the property. In other words, sell and move to a smaller apartment. But why do this when you can lease a part of it or sell the entire property and move to a new country where you can afford the same standard at significantly lower prices? Costa Rica, Panama, Colombia, and Malaysia are excellent choices too.

f. Shop for lower costs

Shopping for lower costs is another innovative way to cut down your operational costs efficiently. Across several services, seniors are provided discounts and opportunities. There are tax reliefs, utility discounts, et cetera. You might not believe how much these discounts can help you save until you grab a calculator and do the math. Thirty cents here and $2 there might cut down more than $100 at the end of the month. The benefit is not just a $100 cut. It is $100 available for next month when you would have another $100 deduction.

With fewer bills at the end of every month and multiple sources of income, there is no limit to how much comfort you can enjoy in the final lapse of your life- which is precisely what I hope to help you achieve with this book. I hope I have succeeded.

9
SMART RETIREMENT
INVESTMENTS

The biggest risk of all is not taking one
– Mellody Hobson

Throughout the seventh chapter, I stressed several investment options that can help you grow your money slowly and consistently. What if you have a considerable amount and you are looking to grow astronomically?

As you may observe, all the investment options discussed recently require little to no capital to start. Some come with loans (such as real estate rental mortgage), and others require moderate capital (think affiliate/networking marketing, blogging, et cetera.) But you may not need them because you are wealthy already. You are only looking for a way to preserve your money such that at the end of the day, you will never have to work at retirement.

If that sounds like you, then this chapter is for you. In the following lines, you will find out some practical ways to achieve a considerable retirement income in the last quarter of your life.

1. Consider Angel Investing

In the observation of a senior financial advisor and sales manager at Merrill Lynch, Tiffany Lam-Balfour, "Angel investing is a type of private equity investing. Here, high net worth investors attempt to earn higher returns by taking on more risk than investing in the public markets." Here is the picture: assuming you are an experienced business owner or a C-level officer (chief executive, chief of finance, and other chief positions), one of the innovative ways to invest your money is to put it into another company through angel investing.

In nearly all cases, the company in which you invest is still in its earliest stage of growth. It has had no investors, and it is actively looking for some. The business may not even have customers yet. It may not have generated any revenue either. However, the business leaders come across as people who know what they are doing and have a feasible plan with a viable product. Moreso, they may have completed a beta test already. But they don't have it all figured out yet. They are just bristling with a lot of promise. Because the business comes across as full of potential, you may invest in them.

The first rule of angel investing is that you must either be highly experienced in that field or work closely with someone who is. You don't have to be in the same industry. But you must understand how business works. You should be smart enough to tell apart a potential hotshot from potential hogwash. You should have a perfect understanding of how to predict progress trends and determine the market response.

With your experience, you should be able to identify a good product and determine whether the business managers are reliable. It is wise to set a very high standard when determining whether the business plan and its executors meet your criteria before making any investments.

A typical angel investor does not expect an instant reward. They finance a business at a time all its hopes of survival hinge on the conviction of the angel investor. A study by UpCounsel, a legal platform, suggests that across the world, the typical investment of angel investors sits between $15,000 and $250,000, although it can vary significantly. Usually, angel investors contribute a relatively small amount of capital to a startup company.

In exchange, the typical angel investor gets between 20% and 50% of the company's stake. The equity dwindles as more investors come on board, but the value of each stake rises, and you make more money.

The saying is that only "family and fools invest in startups." This is not far from reality. Empirical studies by Sean Bryant reveal that 90% of startups failed in 2019, with 21.5% failure recorded in the first year, 30% in the second, and 50% by the fifth year. By the 10th year, 70% of startups would have failed.

Typical reasons for failure include insufficient financing, inability to capture the market, poor research, inadequate collaboration, poor marketing, and lack of expertise in the industry. It is needful to ascertain the likelihood of the chosen business overcoming all these challenges that may beset a startup before making any investment.

You must understand that angel investing is a high-risk, high-reward investment journey. With only a 10% success rate, startups are dicey for your investments. It gets more awkward when you remember that this is not just your wealth creation investment, it is for retirement. So, you should critically evaluate the entity and seek professional opinions before taking a final stand.

Angel investing may require the business managers to seek your opinions and approval in many cases, but you are not actively involved unless you agree to be part of the contract agreement. The business only has to boom, and you can generate ten times your investment or beyond, depending on how successful the firm becomes. To generate profit for you, the company has to make a profit and increase in value, implying that you will be entitled to dividends and a rise in stock value.

Of recent, the fastest rising sectors are core tech and tech businesses (edtech, fintech, microblogging platform, social media, et cetera). "Technology ranks the best among all sectors on our quality metrics, ranking at or near the top for all factors we evaluated," says market strategists at the RBC Capital Markets while describing their 2022 outlook. It is not surprising that despite making so much wealth, the top five most affluent men in the world are all into technology.

If you consider angel investing extremely dicey, consider switching to seed funding.

What is the difference?

Seed investing is an advanced stage of angel investing. This time, the business already has a going market, and it has had angel investments. It is only looking to expand its market with more capital. The likelihood of the business survival is now higher, and it seems safer to invest in the business. At this point, your profits will be fewer than that of angel investors, but that is not surprising as you have fewer risks and the rule that 'the higher the risk, the higher the yield' stands.

With seed investing, there is no guarantee that the business will not fail. A business can fail at any point. The big task is to distinguish a company that can generate profit from those that are unstable.

Consider meeting an investment advisor or signing up for mentorship on angel investing. You may also consult investment bankers, who are professionals that can help you decide where to pump the money. Once you have made the right decision, you then need to sit back and receive constant updates on the yield of your company. There is no limit to how much you can make here.

2. Public Equity

As the direct opposite of private equity, public equity is a way of investing in a public company. Remember that a public company is listed on an exchange market such as the London Exchange, the New York exchange, et cetera. Public equities are accessible by anyone. Unless you own staggering stakes, you can be a passive member; invest your money and follow the trends closely.

One primary advantage of public stocks is that it allows you to invest in less risky ventures. While any company can capsize, public companies are less likely to experience it. Also, it is significantly easier to pull your stakes out of a public business than a private business. A critical point to note here is that a private company may offer publicly traded and privately traded equity, but in such cases, the private equities are not accessible to everyone. It sometimes comes first, and it requires a massive contribution from each investor. Public equities require fewer contributions.

Like the private equity system, you generate wealth in public equity when dividends are shared, and stocks rise in value. You do not need a degree to invest in either. You however require reliable investment analytical skills.

3. Entrepreneurship

Would you rather not invest in other people's businesses? Then entrepreneurship might be the way to go. As explained by the world's biggest Edtech platform, Byju, "entrepreneurship is the ability and readiness to develop, organize, and run a business enterprise along with any of its uncertainties to make a profit." Succinctly put, this is all about developing the ability to set up a system and solve a problem for people.

Typically, entrepreneurship is a perfect blend of innovation, risk, visualization, and organization. This may be complex for you if you are just looking to make yields. But it is not less important. Being an entrepreneur is to bring in something your world needs, strongly believe in it, take the risk, and organize it realistically.

So, if you are looking to become an entrepreneur, this is one crucial part you must prepare for. Earlier, I hinted to you that entrepreneurship is a perilous venture. Up to 90% of startups fail, and you need to have a lot of guts before venturing. Entrepreneurship requires a blend of passion and effort. Fortunately, there are strategic ways to start small such that without plunging a significant amount out of your pension, you can start a small business and make money.

Here are some of the smallest and smartest businesses that require little to no capital to set up.

a. Freelancing

Freelancing is the most convenient way to venture into business in the 21st century. As a free-lancer, you offer services to people across varying industries, meaning that you are no longer tied to a workplace and are independent. If you choose to be a graphic designer, you can apply to take on a few graphic designing roles in more than one company. Once the project is done, you can move on to the next company.

This implies that you can choose who to work with and what to work on. You can equally decide where or when to work. Freelancing allows you to continue offering the services you love when you may not stand a chance with the traditional system. For instance, as a 70-year-old retired programmer, you can reach out to companies worldwide and take up enough projects at your preferred price. Fiverr, PeoplePerHour, Freelancer, and Upwork are thriving freelancing platforms as of 2022.

Freelancing does not offer you the security of a job, income, or pension. But you can decide your charge on each project and you can also continue to provide your expertise upon retirement.

You should also note that you can offer services different from your main occupation before retirement. To provide such services, you may require some form of training. Common freelance services to consider include arts and illustration, print design, proofreading and editing, book design, digital marketing, voice-over services, speech writing, app creation, web programming services, transcription, research and summaries, resume writing, translation services, video editing, creation of subtitles and captions, songwriting, beat making, architecture and interior design, cyber security and data protection services, games development, project management, LinkedIn profile creation, virtual assistant services, and life coaching among many others.

Here are some helpful tips on freelancing by Jamie Johnson who went from earning $8 per hour at Starbucks to making $10,000 - $12,000 monthly as a copywriter on Upwork. First, as a freelancer, you should be ready to start small. You should be willing to accept 'small jobs' as this can go a long way in helping to build your clientele and open up better opportunities eventually. Also, consistency is highly vital in freelancing. You may not be the best video editor or resume writer, but meeting deadlines, responding to emails promptly, and delivering top-notch customer service will definitely set you apart from others.

b. Video content creation

The world is evolving and new lucrative jobs are being created, thanks to the advent of technology. Video content creation involves the sharing of videos on the internet and across various social media platforms such as YouTube, Instagram, TikTok, and Twitch.

Videos serve as important tools to engage your audience, market products and share stories, among others.

As of 2022, Statista reported that the average internet user spends a whopping 147 minutes on social media every day. Data from the Global Web Index showed that the average individual spends nearly 7 hours daily using the internet across all devices. When you consider these numbers, you can begin to understand how people can build niche audiences across these platforms.

YouTube alone has over 2.5 billion active users and over 800 million videos as of 2022 while a newer platform like TikTok hit 1 billion users in the third quarter of 2021 and is even projected to reach 1.8 billion by end of 2022. Other major platforms include Facebook, Twitter, and Instagram. These all have millions and billions of users and serve as sources of revenue generation for many people.

You may wonder if making and uploading videos can fetch a sizable income. The answer is yes. These platforms offer the opportunity of earning money based on the number of views and subscribers and have served as a full-time source of income for many people. YouTube, for example, pays an average of $2 to $5 for every 1000 views of paid advertisement. Other platforms also offer monetary rewards for advertisements made on your videos. If you have very engaging content with many views, you can earn consistently from more than one platform. You also stand a chance for companies contacting you directly for the advertisement of their products. Take a look at the famous footballer, Cristiano Ronaldo who is currently the most followed person on Instagram with over 450 million followers. He earns over $800,000 for each product advertised on his Instagram page.

You should bear in mind that this field is highly competitive and a clear strategy is required to succeed. Kris Collins, a video content creator who began her career during the pandemic lockdown and succeeded in growing her audience to more than 43 million viewers across YouTube, TikTok, Instagram, and Twitch has shared some useful tips. To be successful, you should develop a content strategy. You should also study which population appreciates and watches your content, what time of the day they tend to watch your videos and which type of videos get the highest number of views. These statistics will serve as a guide to creating the right type of content that will enable you to grow your audience exponentially.

There is room to have more than one channel and several niches, but the goal is to have quality content and properly engage your audience.

Are you the reserved type and do not wish to be known? You can still create and upload quality and profitable videos without being physically part of it. Some niches to consider if you prefer this option include cooking tutorials, sleep-enhancing/relaxation videos, product unboxing videos, time-lapse videos, and commentary videos, to mention a few. There is no hard and fast rule regarding the length of the video. It is based on your chosen niche and target audience. You may consider signing up for video content creation courses to learn the required skills for shooting quality videos from your mobile device, video editing, and more.

c. Consultancy

Consultancy is another brilliant venture you can consider. As the name suggests, it is a business system where agencies and less experienced professionals in your niche consult you when they have a complex project. Assuming you retired as a civil engineer with expertise in road construction, government agencies and private entities looking to embark on road projects can consult you for experienced direction. Younger engineers on the job can also consult you.

The primary resource you need to be a consultant is the bank of experience that your years on the job have offered to you. Simultaneously, you have to stay conversant with the trends of your industry so that your suggestions will be relevant. Being a consultant is not significantly different from being a teacher. This time, you relate your teachings to a specialized audience and situation which offers more income.

Being a consultant is an incredible way to pass your last quarter. You can set up a consultancy office in your home. You can rent an office space, and you may consider setting up as a consultant on a freelance platform. You will however need to contact a few marketers for adverts and publicity.

You can continue to work as a project manager, program manager, or even an analyst, depending on your health, experience, and the resources you bring to the table.

d. General trades

Among other options, you can head into general trade and merchandise. As the anonymous saying goes, "everything is money. It depends on who is looking at it and how." You only have to look around, and you will realize what could turn into business for you. Considering your age and energy, you may not want to go into full-fledged production. It is healthier and less stressful to ship or order products from large companies and sell to neighboring communities.

It might seem as though we can sell every product on impulse until you factor in the rules of selecting a product to sell. The primary rule, in this case, is that you ensure that you bring value to the table. The product or service you choose to sell must be scarce and required. It must also be less strenuous to deliver, and it has to be profitable for you. When you put these factors together, you will realize that only a few products satisfactorily tick the box. It requires critical analysis.

When you finally find a product, you can sell from home, rent a space for shipment, or even work as a drop shipper online. The important note is to pick a product with a market you can reach. You also need to learn several business and marketing models and what may or may not work for you.

Should you intend to set up a large business, consider hiring someone to run the place. This is because entrepreneurship is naturally time-consuming and demanding. Be free from any overwhelming activity that reduces your time for yourself, healthcare, et cetera. There is no limit to how wealthy entrepreneurship can make you.

AFTERWORD

Retirement is one of the most exciting times of life. It allows you to relax, catch up with friends and family and fulfill your bucket list.

Many people look forward to retirement but do not realize they are ill-prepared for this important phase. While some retire with huge debts, others invest in unprofitable ventures. Some people even save up lump sums of money that they hope to spend all through retirement. The trouble is that despite what they have planned for years, statistics prove that many retirees still cannot foot their bills. They have worked themselves out, so working harder is not the question. It is a question of working smarter.

This book has shared several pragmatic ways of

generating smart retirement income that will ensure your bills are paid and you can have enough to spare.

Should you require further clarifications, feel free to contact me and my team via this email address – christine.bpierce@gmail.com. I will also appreciate your feedback.

BIBLIOGRAPHY

- Eric P. (2021, September 13). A Guide to the common retirement stages and what to expect. Wildpine Residence. Available at: https://wildpineresidence.ca/the-5-stages-of-retirement-everyone-will-go-through/

- Ananya, B. (2022, March 16). 145 Funny Retirement Quotes for coworkers, friends, and family. Available at: https://www.therandomvibez.com/funny-retirement-quotes-sayings-one-liners/

- Retirement 2021. In *Merriam-Webster.com*. Available at: https://www.merriam-webster.com/dictionary/retirement

- Jeff, H. (2022, May 6) 30 Retirement Quotes. Senior Living Organization. Available at: https://www.seniorliving.org/retirement/quotes/

- Ziprecruiter (2022, December 13). Average Annual Salary. Available at: https://www.ziprecruiter.co.uk/?utm_source=zr-go-redirect

- Charles Weeks (2017, June 22). Mark Twain on Regrets, Learning from Legends. Unbroke. Available at: https://unbroke.net/twain-regrets-retirement/

BIBLIOGRAPHY

- Jessica, D. (2022, February 17) Despite Rising Wages, 61% of Americans are still living paycheck to paycheck. CNBC. Available at: https://www.cnbc.com/2022/02/17/wages-are-rising-but-many-americans-still-live-paycheck-to-paycheck.html

- Quote Fancy. (2017, November 25) Jonathan Clements Quote. Available at: https://quotefancy.com/quote/1648389/Jonathan-Clements-Retirement-is-like-a-long-vacation-in-Las-Vegas-The-goal-is-to-enjoy-it

- PwC. (2017, August 4). Retirement in America: Time to Rethink. Available at: https://www.pwc.com/us/en/industries/financial-services/library/retirement-in-america.html

- Brittany King (2022, January 13) Women more likely than men to have no retirement savings. Available at: https://www.census.gov/library/stories/2022/01/women-more-likely-than-men-to-have-no-retirement-savings.html

- Zagorsky, J. (2005). Marriage and Divorces Impact on Wealth. Journal of Sociology - J SOCIOL. 41. 406-424. 10.1177/1440783305058478.

- Andrew, B. (2020, January 27) Factcheck: Do 40% of Retirees rely on Social Security for their Entire Income? Forbes. Available at: https://www.forbes.

com/sites/andrewbiggs/2020/01/27/factcheck-do-40-of-retirees-rely-on-social-security-for-their-entire-income/

- Victoria J. Haneman. (2019). Intergenerational Equity, Student Loan Debt, and Taxing Rich Dead People. Bluebook 20th ed.

- Sunlife Canada (2015, February 18) Working Canadians are much more worried than retirees about running out of money. Available at: https://www.newswire.ca/news-releases/working-canadians-are-much-more-worried-than-retirees-about-running-out-of-money-516902771.html

- Rajeshni, N. (2018, February 24) The not so golden years- a quarter of retired Canadians in debt, Survey suggests. CBC News. Available at: https://www.cbc.ca/news/business/canadians-retirement-debt-1.4547125

- Senior Living Organization. (2021, April 27). Getting out of Debt: A guide for aging adults. Available at: https://www.seniorliving.org/research/getting-out-of-debt/

- Jimenez Law Firm. (2021, August 18). How finances affect divorce rates in America. Available at: https://thejimenezlawfirm.com/how-finances-affect-divorce-rates-in-america/

BIBLIOGRAPHY

- Morgan, S. (2018, November 20). Stop Giving Your Money to the Bank: Save Smarter and Save the World. Forbes. Available at: https://www.forbes.com/sites/morgansimon/2018/11/20/stop-giving-your-money-to-the-bank-save-smarter-and-change-the-world-too/

- Andrew, B. (2022, April 11). Simple ways to invest in real estate. Investopedia. Available at: https://www.investopedia.com/investing/simple-ways-invest-real-estate/

- Barclay, P. (2022, April 7). Key Reasons to Invest in Real Estate. Investopedia. Available at: https://www.investopedia.com/articles/mortgages-real-estate/11/key-reasons-invest-real-estate.asp

- Healthy Aging team. (2021, April). The Top 10 Most Common Chronic Conditions in Older Adults. National Council on Aging. Available at: https://www.ncoa.org/article/the-top-10-most-common-chronic-conditions-in-older-adults

- Statista. (2022, May). Financial Instruments owned by children in the United States 2022. Available at: https://www.statista.com/statistics/542668/financial-instruments-owned-by-kids-usa/

- Eastman M.B. (2022, June 2). Online Banking Vs. Traditional Banking - Which Is Better For You? Money Under 30. Available at: https://www.

moneyunder30.com/online-banking-vs-
traditional-banking

- McWhinney J. (2021, December 20). 5 Mistakes
  That Can Make House Flipping a Flop.
  Investopedia. Available at: https://www.
  investopedia.com/articles/mortgages-real-estate/
  08/house-flip.asp

- Chen J. (2022, April 4) Real Estate Investment
  Trust (REIT) Investopedia. Available at: https://
  www.investopedia.com/terms/r/reit.asp

- Worth J. (2021, September 29). New Morningstar
  analysis shows the optimal allocation to REITS.
  Nareit. Available at: https://www.reit.com/news/
  blog/market-commentary/new-morningstar-
  analysis-shows-optimal-allocation-reits

- DiLallo M, (2022, March 24). REITs vs Stocks:
  What Does the Data Say? The Motley Fool.
  Available at: https://www.fool.com/research/reits-
  vs-stocks/

- Konrad Soipelinikow. (2021). A Beginner's Guide
  To Buy & Hold Real Estate. Fortune Builders.
  Available at: https://www.fortunebuilders.com/a-
  beginners-guide-to-buy-hold-real-estate/

- James Chen (2022, April 4). Real Estate
  Investment Trust (REIT). Investopedia. Available

at: https://www.investopedia.com/terms/r/
reit.asp

- Brandon E. (2018, February 26). Why More
  Retirees Are Becoming Renters. U.S. News and
  World Report. Available at: https://money.usnews.
  com/money/retirement/baby-boomers/articles/
  why-more-retirees-are-becoming-renters#:.

- Brumer-Smith L. (2022, June 10) How REIGs
  work and if they're right for you. The Motley Fool.
  Available at: https://www.fool.com/investing/
  stock-market/market-sectors/real-estate-investing/
  basics/real-estate-investment-group/

- Araj V. (2021, December 23) What Is House
  Hacking And Is It Something You Should Be
  Doing? Rocket Mortgage. Available at: https://
  www.rocketmortgage.com/learn/house-hacking

- Rohde J. (n.d.) The pros and cons of owning
  multiple properties. Stessa. Available at: https://
  www.stessa.com/blog/owning-multiple-
  properties/

- Olito F & Gal S. (2019, June 10) Here's what the
  average American family of four spends on rent in
  every state. Business Insider. Available at: https://
  www.businessinsider.in/heres-what-the-average-
  american-family-of-four-spends-on-rent-in-every-
  state/articleshow/69731246.cms

BIBLIOGRAPHY

- Winck B. (2021, July 2) Your rents are going to keep going up. Business Insider. Available at: https://www.businessinsider.com/rent-inflation-housing-market-real-estate-shelter-price-growth-outlook-2021-7?r=US&IR=T

- Duffin E. (2022, January 14) Share of K-12 students in the United States who use digital learning tools daily in 2019, by school level. Statista. Available at: https://www.statista.com/statistics/1076292/share-k-12-students-us-who-use-digital-learning-tools-daily-level/ _

- What is a Blog and How is it Different from a Website? (Explained) (2022) WPBeginner. Available at: https://www.wpbeginner.com/beginners-guide/what-is-a-blog-and-how-is-it-different-from-a-website-explained/#:

- Oulette C. (2022, April 22) Ultimate List of Blogging Statistics and Facts (Updated for 2022) Optinmonster. Available at: https://optinmonster.com/blogging-statistics/

- Kindle: A year in review (2019, December 23) Amazon. Available at: https://www.aboutamazon.co.uk/news/innovation/kindle-a-year-in-review

- National Priorities Project. Borrowing and the Federal Debt. Available at: https://www.

nationalpriorities.org/budget-basics/federal-budget-101/borrowing-and-federal-debt/

- Frankenfield J. (2022, July 5) Affiliate Marketing. Investopedia. Available at: https://www.investopedia.com/terms/a/affiliate-marketing.asp#:

- Tarver E. (2022, July 25) Multilevel Marketing (MLM) Investopedia. Available at: https://www.investopedia.com/terms/m/multi-level-marketing.asp

- Lam-Balfour T. (2022, April 12) Angel Investing: What It Is and How to Start. Nerdwallet. Available at: https://www.nerdwallet.com/article/investing/angel-investing

- How Much Do Angel Investors Usually Invest? UpCounsel. Available at: https://www.upcounsel.com/how-much-do-angel-investors-usually-invest

- Mandal P. (2022, January 6) These were the 5 Best Performing Tech Stocks of 2021. StockNews. Available at: https://stocknews.com/news/clfd-aehr-fcuv-auid-trt-these-were-the-5-best-performing-tech-stocks-of-2021/

- Byju's. Entrepreneurship–Types of Entrepreneurship. Available at: https://byjus.com/commerce/what-is-entrepreneurship/

BIBLIOGRAPHY

- Marr B. (2022, April 29) How To Become A Successful Video Content Creator – Insights From KallmeKris. Forbes. Available at: https://www.forbes.com/sites/bernardmarr/2022/04/29/how-to-become-a-successful-video-content-creator--insights-from-kallmekris/

- Statista. (2022). Daily time spent on social networking by internet users worldwide from 2012 to 2022. https://www.statista.com/statistics/433871/daily-social-media-usage-worldwide/